See, There He Is
a memoir

GINGER GRAZIANO

Copyright ©2015 by Ginger Graziano

ISBN 978-0-9908986-0-3
Library of Congress Control Number: 2014918591

No part of this publication may be reproduced, stored in a retrieval system, or transmitted in any form or by any means, electronic, mechanical, photocopying, recording, scanning, or otherwise, except as permitted under Section 107 or 108 of the 1978 United States Copyright Act, without the prior written permission of the author. Requests may be made through the publisher, Free Bird Press, 54 Tremont Street, Asheville, North Carolina 28806.

The author is grateful to the following magazines and anthologies for publishing pieces from *See, There He Is*. "Exact Change Speeds Trips" was published in *Embodied Effigies* from Ball State University. "Sweat" was published in *Stone Voices/Shanti Arts*. "Bless the Ice Cream," "Sloan Kettering," and "Breakdown" were published in the anthology *Writing in Circles*.

Text set in Adobe Garamond
Designed by Ginger Graziano
www.gingergraziano.com

Printed in the United States of America

Cover image: isoga/Shutterstock, Inc.
Author's photo: Max Poppers

Free Bird Press
Asheville, NC 28806

for
Jennifer
and
Jeremy

See, There He Is

New York City—2010

Memories lie.

They follow well-worn pathways, creating stories from bits and pieces of remembered life. My daughter, Jenny, recalls events in such detail that I wonder if I saw only what I wanted to see.

Our trip north to New York for her bridal shower becomes an adventure in falling back in time. Driving the New Jersey Turnpike at midnight after twelve hours on the road, I see the lights of Manhattan. "There's my city," I say, surprised by how much emotion arises. New York seemed to exist only in my past but here it is alive, real. Nine years ago the towers fell, yet I still see the hole in the skyline where they stood just as I feel the space in my heart where Jeremy used to be.

I have returned with Jenny to the place we both left, she first and then I a few years later. We moved south because we could no longer live with Jeremy's absence.

I enter my past, not through the eyes of my old hurts and losses—but clean and curious, with new eyes. Was I missing something then, fresh from my loss, unable to grasp what I see now? Or, am I experiencing it as the mother of the bride, through Jenny's life and her memories, blessed by the joy in our family?

Every area I visit holds memory for me—all the years of my youth and young married life on to the time alone with my children.

I borrow Jenny's car the day before her bridal shower and drive up the hill into Sea Cliff, past the house I lived in with Jeremy the last two years of his life when we sought sanctuary from the storm of his illness. New people live here, but gulls still wheel over Long Island Sound. The Welwyn Preserve's paths are overgrown. I walk them anyway, remembering.

Now, though, it's a joyous occasion, as my Jewish friends call it: a *barakh*. A wedding. My daughter brings joy to us all—new hope, maybe a child, certainly a loved son-in-law. After all the years of family leaving and diminishing, the tide has turned. I have come back to claim better memories and join the family of mothers preparing their daughters for a rite of passage.

The sea sparkles in the morning sun. I see it from the Throgs Neck Bridge, fading off into the far distance.

DREAM

It scares me when I wake to dread. It scares me to think of those I love dying.

Before Jeremy got sick I dreamed he had died. I woke sobbing.

For a long time I tried to push this out of my mind. My journal entry for that day, only one sentence. Nothing more to say. Throat clenched, no other words could come through.

Years before, I dreamed I stood on a high hill overlooking the water holding my two childrens' hands. One of them was swept away. I could never see which one. This dream recurred many times. I thought, it's only a dream. *A deeper part of me said* no.

I couldn't listen.

No.

No.

I dreamed the towers fell before they did.

PART I
1991-1993

Bayside, NY—1991

BANG

"Come on!" I yelled from the bottom of the stairs. "We're going to be late for my opening."

I watched Jeremy struggle into his jacket as he closed the door. "I'm late because she wouldn't get out of the bathroom."

"Oh, stop it," Jenny said. "You're always late." She tossed her long hair. "I'm surprised you turned off your video game and left your room," she called back as she ran down the stairs, her high heels clicking.

One of my paintings hung in the Queens College show that my art group, Alliance of Queens Artists, had been invited to, and I felt my artistic life begin to unfold. Although I worked as a graphic designer, my college degree was in fine arts. Jeremy had started his last year of high school and Jenny was temporarily back home while working in Manhattan. My years of single parenting were coming to fruition as I watched them move into their own lives.

In the driveway I unlocked my red Honda and stepped aside as Jeremy scooted around me, Jenny behind him. She pushed him forward impatiently as he ducked his head to get into the back seat, slamming the right side of his head into the door frame. He yelled in pain.

I looked at his head, rubbed the spot. No bruise or bump.

They both scrambled into the back seat. As I turned to back out, I noticed him touching his head.

The next day he began having headaches and came home from school early. The doctor diagnosed a concussion and reassured us that he would recover in a few days. It seemed odd to me that the bump on his head was strong enough to cause a concussion. I had seen Jenny push him. It hadn't seemed that hard, but I was angry and blamed her.

I planned a four-day vacation to Montauk after the weekend to decide what to do about my partner, Paul. We had lived together for more than two years. Our relationship had deteriorated into screaming fights and the kind of bickering that resolves nothing. Since my mother's death a year and a half before, grief had taken all my focus. Recently, however, as the sadness lifted, I questioned, *do I want to stay with Paul?*

Jeremy remained in bed for three days, not eating much. I placed ice packs on his head, hoping to relieve the pain. He lay with one arm over his eyes, moaning. Calls to the doctor brought assurance that concussions took time to heal.

On Saturday when I returned from my gallery-sitting shift at Queens College, I looked up at his window. He waited for me. I waved. He put his hand on the glass and leaned his head against it.

On Sunday he fell into a deep sleep and slept for hours, which I interpreted as a sign that he was starting to heal, but later that evening I couldn't wake him. His body felt cold and he'd wet the bed. I half carried, half dragged him into the bathroom, sure a warm bath would help. I stripped off his wet pajamas and helped him into the tub. I hadn't seen my son naked in years. Thinking he needed privacy, I handed him soap and left the room, reconsidered, and went back in. He was slumped over the side of the tub, unconscious.

I had to get him to the emergency room of North Shore University Hospital immediately. Jenny and I dressed him while he hung limp as a rag doll. Paul drove while Jenny stayed behind to call the doctor and alert her and Jeremy's father, Vinny. The car seemed to move in slow motion.

I kept thinking, *this can't be happening!*

When I saw the white amoeba-like blob on the CT scan of Jeremy's head, I didn't understand what it meant. I was alone when the doctor told me the scan indicated a brain tumor. My legs buckled and I fell to the floor.

When Vinny arrived, the surgeon called us into another room for a conference and said they had to operate or he'd die. The tumor was bleeding, causing his brain to swell. The pressure would kill him.

I grasped his hands. "Please, please operate immediately!"

In the emergency room Jeremy was semi-conscious, his left leg shaking uncontrollably. He moaned over and over, "When are they going to operate?"

All night we waited on plastic chairs in the sterile empty hospital corridor, keeping vigil—Jenny, Paul, Vinny, and me. No one spoke. *What was there to say?* Jenny sat next to me on my left. I don't know if I reached out to comfort her. I was lost in shock.

We waited for the verdict, thought of Jeremy lying somewhere close by with his head opened like a flower, the seeds of the journey we were undertaking already ripe and glowing.

Loudspeaker announcements with undecipherable messages broke the silence. We were still half asleep within our old life—the one that seemed so simple now—the one that we had even been bored with. We sat against the wall on the longest night I have ever experienced. Even though we didn't talk, we took comfort in being together. Occasionally I would leap ahead in my mind, only to scurry back in fear to the cold corridor, the hard chairs, the last moments of hope.

Finally the surgeon walked down the hall, still dressed in green scrubs, and told us they removed as much of the tumor as possible. *What did this mean?* Jeremy was coming around. We could see him soon.

They wheeled him to the ICU and later called us in.

His legs were swaddled in pressure bandages, his head wrapped in gauze. A clear plastic bottle attached to the top of his head oozed a pinkish-red liquid. I stared at the breathing tube that protruded from his mouth. As he began to wake up, he gagged, fighting to get the tube out. I grabbed his arm. "Jeremy, don't fight it." Then I started to fall.

The nurses and Vinny pulled me into the corridor. I was shaking and crying. My son was so sick, no longer the Jeremy I had known three days ago.

We waited outside the ICU. I found a phone in the hallway, called my friend Esther, and also told my boss I wouldn't be in. Then Jenny ran to tell me that he had woken up. I raced back to the ICU.

He was propped up in bed, joking with his visitors, the tube removed. I walked over and hugged him. He looked as if he had woken from a good night's sleep. This was the Jeremy I knew, except that with his head wrapped in bandages, he looked like a casualty of war.

Jeremy's laughter told me he was happy to have awakened and be without pain. He had come through a dark passage and now he was okay. *Everything would be fine again, right?*

Jenny looked on, relieved that the reason for her brother's pain was not the result of her push. In fact her push alerted us to the silent tumor growing in his head. We were shocked that in the space of four days our familiar world had slid away, revealing life's unpredictability.

SHATTER

Despite his bravado, Jeremy was frightened. "I'm staying tonight," I told him. "I'll be across the hall in case you need me." He nodded his head.

I had drifted into exhausted sleep on a plastic chair in the waiting room, my feet propped on the coffee table, when a nurse tapped me. I came awake with a start, not remembering where I was. Jeremy was calling for me.

He was propped up in bed. The fluorescent light on the wall behind the bed cast a ghostly glow. "I can't sleep," he said.

I sat down on the bedside chair and took his hand. He looked trapped, wired to all the hospital equipment, his legs still wrapped in pressure bandages.

"What's going to happen to me?" I heard the fear in his voice.

I wasn't sure what to say. My head was spinning from the last twenty-four hours. My own scared thoughts ricocheted in my brain. "We're going to get through this. Let's see what the doctors say in the morning. Everyone…"

"I'm scared."

"I know." I felt him shaking beneath my hand. I stroked his arm. I focused on being present with him, the only thing that made any sense. He was breathing hard. I continued to stroke his arm, his damp hand clasped in mine. I was being called to the hardest challenge I ever faced in my life. I knew I would be there for him in any way I could.

"Let's just breathe, Jeremy." He gripped my hand tighter. "Let's just try to relax a little. I'm here. I love you. We'll deal with this." Over and over I said words like this, pledging that I would be there to walk this road with him, as we breathed into the first night of our shattered world.

THE DOCTORS WERE AMAZED AT JEREMY'S RAPID RECOVERY AND released him after a week. Love and support continued to pour in. When Jeremy left the hospital with bandages still on his head, he left behind his innocence, his belief that his body could carry him anywhere he wanted. Maybe he wouldn't get his peripheral vision back, or maybe his head would always feel bruised, tender, invaded.

He came home, but I could see by his tentative steps as he entered the hallway that everything looked different, like a place he hadn't seen for a long time. He walked into his room. So much had happened in a week, maybe it was no longer his safe haven. He scanned his TV, books, and games as he pivoted. He sat on his bed, the one he had peed in the day I finally realized something was wrong.

I had made his favorite foods, veal cutlets and mashed potatoes, and although he was hungry, he couldn't settle enough to eat. He wandered through the rooms. Bonnie wagged her tail. "Hey, butthead," he said. In the bathroom he picked up his hairbrush and looked at his shaven head. I wondered if he could push back his fear and ever feel safe in his own body again.

I stood in the kitchen doorway watching him. Neither of us knew what to say. Nothing felt solid. Nothing.

He sat down on the sofa and leaned back against its cushions. It held him up for now.

Jenny was still at work. She would come home that evening and her brother would be back in his place. When she walked in, she fell into their familiar routine of banter, but instead of sharp funny comments, she was uncharacteristically gentle.

INNOCENCE

WE CAME HOME WITH A FALSE SENSE OF SECURITY. THE NEUROLOGIST on Jeremy's case thought he had a rare benign tumor, but wanted us to get a second opinion at Sloan-Kettering in New York City.

Four of us—Vinny; his wife, Kyle; Paul; and me—went for our appointment with Dr. Walker, four supplicants for the life of Jeremy. She cut right to the point, told us that Jeremy had an ugly cancerous tumor, a stage IV glioma, which had been growing for years until it reached the size where a bump on his head caused it to hemorrhage. They could offer him radiation, chemotherapy, and radiation implants—the best they could do.

We were silent. Kyle, a trained nurse, burst into tears and ran out of the room. The rest of us sat, stunned. This wasn't what we expected. Dr. Walker wanted to do radiation implants before Thanksgiving.

When the meeting ended we left in silence. We made no small talk as we descended to the cafeteria. The food tasted like cardboard. I could hardly swallow.

I drove home, bringing pizza for Jeremy, holding a terrible secret. *What do I say to him and when?* I wanted Vinny and Kyle to come down from Wilton, Connecticut; we needed to talk as a family. Vinny said, "Hold off. Let's wait." I thought, *for what?*

Both Jeremy and Jenny believed the first diagnosis of a benign tumor was true. Jeremy said, "I'm a simple guy, nothing big ever happens to me, so this is probably a simple tumor."

My children returned to normal. Jenny made the long trip into Manhattan every day. Jeremy rested and healed. My work schedule slowed down before the next magazines were due so I was home more. I made dinner and we ate on the couch. Paul and I still fought.

Ten days passed. I watched my children go along, innocent. I found it physically and emotionally excruciating to not speak the truth.

Finally I drove Jenny and Jeremy to Vinny's, agreeing to spend the night with my friend Robbie who lived in the same town. We gathered in Vinny and Kyle's living room and told the children that Jeremy's tumor was cancerous, not benign. We told him there were treatments he could undergo to fight it, starting with radiation implants. He was quiet. I almost thought he didn't hear us, but he did.

"How do you feel about what we told you, Jeremy?" I asked.

"Come on, don't ask him that," Vinny said.

As usual, our approaches were different.

Vinny and Kyle left for a party that evening, he in a tuxedo and she in a black dress, as if their world was unchanged. Maybe it was. I lingered after they left; I couldn't leave Jeremy or Jenny alone. Jenny babysat for her half-brother and -sister, T.C. and Kane. I heard them talking as she put them to bed. Jeremy watched TV. I wandered through the rooms, wanted to hold my children close to protect them. Maybe they took the news in stride. Maybe it hadn't sunk in yet. Maybe we had presented Jeremy's cancer as if it were fixable. I wasn't sure. I had read the statistics.

Back home, I lay in bed each morning shaking with fear for Jeremy while Paul dressed for work. Despite my obvious distress, he didn't reach out to comfort me. I had nothing to give and that infuriated him. He buried himself in his business, which was faltering.

Bayside, NY—1991

INVADE

I thought back to 1988 when Jenny left home at seventeen. I knew her going was partly because of Paul, brought to a final head the day he rushed into our bedroom asking if I knew Jenny had condoms in her room.

What was he doing snooping around her room? He asked if I was upset about the condoms, but I was more upset that he felt it his right to invade her privacy. She and I had discussed birth control, and I preferred that she protect herself. He wouldn't let up, saying he was going to talk with her. I shook my head, warning him that this was none of his business.

Later that evening Paul cornered Jenny before I had a chance to intervene. Just as well. She could handle herself. Her expression hardened; she was furious. He wasn't her father and had no right to tell her what to do. With that she stormed into her room and slammed the door. Paul looked to me for support. I shrugged my shoulders and walked away. I knew how to talk with Jenny. We respected each other even when we argued.

A few weeks later she came into the kitchen while I cooked dinner and told me that Lisa and she had found an apartment in Sunset Park, Brooklyn, and were moving in together. I put down the spoon and turned to her. "Jen, you're only seventeen and you haven't finished high school yet."

"Paul drives me crazy. I can't live with him," she said. "Besides I have a job as a hostess in the Village so I'll be okay."

Nothing I could do would make this better. She didn't like Paul and he wasn't going to stop trying to control her. I asked her to finish school first, but knew she wasn't listening.

Over the next few weeks I tried to persuade her to stay, even pulled out my last parental card— forbidding her—although I knew she would leave anyway. Paul felt I should force her to stay. I laughed. He obviously didn't know my daughter.

Moving day came. Lisa and her father arrived in a U-Haul van. Silently I helped Jenny move her things downstairs. I worried about her. *Had I taught her everything she needed in order to survive?*

After everything was loaded, I handed her a bag of food—sandwiches, cookies, and soda—in case she got hungry. I saw her struggling with goodbye. She asked if she could come home if it didn't work out.

With tears in my eyes, I told her she could always come home.

I thought about the price I paid to be in relationship with Paul. He maneuvered me into a position where I felt in the middle, a referee between his needs and my children's. I thought of how my mother was always in the middle in our family, protecting my brother and me from our father's anger.

> *On a typical night in our one-bedroom apartment in the Bronx where I grew up, my family sat around three sides of the Formica and chrome table as we ate dinner. The fourth side was pushed against the wall of the narrow kitchen. My father faced me and my mother and brother lined up next to each other.*
>
> *I never knew what the emotional dinner weather would be. My father was volatile; dinner was often heavy with his moods or tantrums. My brother kept to the background, staying out of the line of fire. My father had beaten that into him. My mother watched in case she had to jump in, something she was good at. At sixteen, my loyalties focused on my friends. I visited my family at dinner, but was out or busy otherwise.*
>
> *I don't remember what we ate. Peas if it was Tuesday. The* New York Daily News *rested on the table. Maybe I said something that my father misunderstood. Did he have another bad day at work? His brows knit into two deep lines.* Not good. *His face reddened and he scowled.* Uh-oh, *I thought.*

I pushed my plate away, confused and unable to eat the rest of my dinner. My brother left the room. My father accused me of something—bad behavior or answering him back, one of my favorites. I couldn't seem to help myself. The words just sprang out. He came towards me with the Daily News *rolled up in his hand like a weapon and hit me on my head and shoulders, venting his rage. I gripped the back of the chair and stared at him as he screamed. I was a curious onlooker.*

His tirade ended. I looked at my father, who struck terror in my heart during my whole childhood. "Are you done?" I said.

His face crumpled as if he had been slapped. He dropped the paper and walked out of the kitchen.

He never hit me again.

AFTER JENNY LEFT, I HAD TIME TO FOCUS ON WHAT MY LIFE WAS LIKE with Paul. After he left his studio apartment in Manhattan and moved in with us, I was shocked at how difficult it became to live with him. His need to control everything replaced the easy fun we had at first. I felt permanently stuck in molasses, unable to negotiate even the simplest transactions. He must have felt he had moved to a foreign country and no one understood him. I thought about the admonition: *be careful what you ask for.* The only way I found to diffuse our arguments was to leave the house for an hour until we both calmed down.

IN JANUARY 1991, AFTER MORE THAN TWO YEARS AWAY, JENNY CALLED. Their second apartment in a better neighborhood was too expensive and they owed Lisa's father money. She asked to come home for a while.

I talked to Paul about Jenny's request. He replied that she could come home for three months, but after that she had to find her own place. I refused to ask my daughter to leave to appease Paul, saying that I'd never do that to his children if they asked to live with us.

Jenny arrived and I helped her carry her suitcase and boxes back to her room. She heaved a box of spices and kitchen supplies onto the counter. We found spaces for them in the cabinets.

She was now receptionist for a designer wall-covering firm and left for Manhattan every day. On weekends, she spent time with her friends. She was home, but not around much.

Looking back on this time before Jeremy got sick, I wondered how he felt about the frequent fights he heard from the safety of his room. Paul hollering, "I'm not like this," or "You're cruel and unreasonable." My screams back at him, "Here we go again. Does it ever end?"

Morning light streamed into Jeremy's aqua-painted room. Most hot summer days he slept until noon, having stayed up late the previous night. He holed up in his room, his sanctuary and prison in the house of drama and poisonous energy. He and his sister were no longer allowed to come into our room and hang out on the bed talking. Paul muscled in, so Jeremy retreated. The walls echoed with laughter long gone. The solidarity of our family—the three of us living for years in relative harmony—was shattered. Maybe Paul didn't know how to join in, but control was a bad way. He and Jeremy joked and seemed to have an easy relationship. I think he felt Jeremy was an ally. When we first announced to our four children that we were going to live together, Jeremy took his chair from the living room and moved it close to his room, out of the circle of the rest of us, the action a statement—maybe he didn't want to be part of this family.

> *Jeremy watches TV, plays video games, or still sometimes plays with his Legos or Transformers—toys that change from a car to a powerful hero with just a few flicks of his wrist.*
>
> *Does he wonder if the fighting will go on forever? Will Paul and his mother marry? Does he feel his own foundation melting away, leaving him adrift on the life raft of his room where he can close the door but not close out the angry words or his mother's distress? Sixteen is a tough age, his body in flux, everything changing. He needs a place where he can be the lord. He keeps his room as he*

wants—the captain's bed, formerly a loft bed he slept in high above the ground, now on the floor. From his window he watches us leave or come home, watches the sun move across the sky in its journey down into the dark. He races down the stairs, goes to school, comes home first.

In my imagination I see him get Vienna Fingers and a Coke from the refrigerator and take them into his room. He turns the TV on, picks up his video game, fights to win by gobbling up the enemy, and emerges victorious. Time fades as he enters the game, running down the corridors far from 226th Street in Queens, chasing the enemy, shooting him, leaping over his body, and racing on.

The light was fading as I arrived home. "Hi, Jeremy," I called. He grunted, "Hi." The next video screen came up. He killed all the bad guys, but new ones appeared. I knocked on his door. "Can I come in?"

"Yeah."

I entered and looked at him with his hand on the joystick, flying down the corridors and turning the corner, intent, in another world far from his room.

FREE

Now, after yet another fight with Paul shortly after Jeremy came home from surgery, I asked him why he stayed if he thought I was "cruel and sadistic." Our personalities were so different that we couldn't understand each other's needs. Our difficult relationship, already under stress, couldn't handle Jeremy's illness. I wanted to pick up a knife and hold it to his throat; I had my father's anger. Paul stormed into our bedroom, and after much banging and door slamming, emerged with his suitcase. He called his brother to pick him up. Once he left, I walked our dog in the cold October night, feeling as if a great burden had been lifted.

I was free of him. I realized how infuriating it was to deal with him. After four years he slipped away almost without notice.

Bayside, NY—1991

FREEDOM

I felt Jeremy needed to return to normal as soon as possible after his surgery in order to graduate from high school with his class the following June. As soon as the doctor gave the okay, I arranged for his school to send a tutor so he could keep up with his studies.

With Paul gone, I asked Jenny to contribute every month towards the rent. Otherwise, we would have to move to a smaller apartment. She wasn't happy at first and stormed off to her room, but after a short time emerged to say she would do this. Every month she handed me money before I even asked. She was growing up and taking responsibility.

In the midst of all the turmoil, the company where I freelanced was at risk of losing its biggest client. The client asked us to re-bid the project along with other competitors. I couldn't be out of work, so I spent weekends and nights working to redesign the publication. We made a sensational presentation and won. For now, work was secure.

One Wednesday I took Jeremy and Jenny shopping to a local department store's one-day sale. Paul had taken appliances and other household items when he left and we needed replacements. We acted like the contestants on those TV shows who had an hour in a department store to buy anything they wanted. We had never gone on a shopping spree. I told the children to pick out new sheets and towels for themselves. I rummaged through the pillows, squeezing them for the most comfortable ones, adding four to the almost-full cart. I asked Jenny to get another cart. She laughed and ran off. Jeremy reminded me that we needed new glasses and added square-shaped tumblers to the second cart.

I found a black toaster oven to replace the one Paul had started a fire in. I was sick of looking at those burn streaks.

I could see the joy on Jeremy's face as he picked out CD players for Jenny and me. He used money he'd made working in Waldbaum's supermarket to treat us. Paul had taken his CD player, leaving us no way to play music.

We strolled through the store laughing. I charged our purchases, saying, "Who cares, it's only money!" I wanted us to enjoy more comfort and good things. Why wait? Other shoppers stared as we laughed and danced around. Did they think we'd come into a windfall of money? No, it was better than that. Much better.

We purchased so much that I brought the car around to the entrance to load everything. We were in high spirits. We were alive, we were celebrating, and we were together.

The following week I bought quilts, drapes, and a new dresser for Jeremy. I began repainting the whole apartment. I shampooed the rugs and washed the windows, determined to cleanse my life. Every night I moved furniture and painted walls until two. I wanted every hint of Paul gone.

One Friday night when Jeremy and Jenny were with Vinny for the weekend, I painted the kitchen a warm terra cotta, and cried for what was happening to Jeremy, for my hard years of struggle as a single parent, and the harshness of where I found myself. How had this become my life? How could this be happening to Jeremy? I was beaten down, ashamed of all these tragedies. I felt like Job. How much more could we take?

Jeremy's Beginning—1974

BIRTH

For the first two days after Jeremy was born, his name was Jonathan. Every time I looked at his little screwed-up red face screaming until veins popped out on his temples, I thought, No.

His father wanted to name him after himself, which I vehemently opposed. I wanted him to have his own identity.

We hadn't gotten around to girls' names. Just as well since he turned out to be a boy. While I was in labor, we still pored over the baby name books, unable to agree. Now I could throw them away, no need anymore. I wasn't having any more babies with Vinny.

We still couldn't agree on a name although we both felt Jonathan wasn't right. Our second choice was Jeremy. I had hoped for a boy since we already had Jenny. One of each. Complete.

His mouth opened wide like a little bird, such a primal instinct— screaming for food. The ones that survive scream the loudest.

I stared at him every time the nurse brought him to me. I couldn't imagine whom I'd given birth to. He resembled no one I knew except maybe a frantic little nestling. My daughter had opened her eyes right away and looked around. He looked as if he didn't want to be here, his eyes scrunched tight against the world.

He was off the hospital's four-hour feeding schedule, and although I was breastfeeding, the nurses refused to bring him to me when he cried.

Outside the nursery I watched him cry, his face red, with the glass between us.

I walked up to the nurse on duty. "Let me feed my baby."

"*No, it's not feeding time.*"

"*Look at him screaming!*" *I couldn't stand watching him. It was tearing me apart. When they did bring him to me, he'd guzzle furiously and then fall into an exhausted sleep. He hadn't eaten* enough. I couldn't wake him though I tried, even pinching him in my desperation. The nurse arrived to take him back to the nursery.

On the third day I called Vinny. "I'm leaving this fucking place. You'd better come and get us before I take Jeremy and walk out."

"Wait a minute," he said. "Calm down. Let me call the doctor first."

"Fine. Do that, but you'd better come and get us right now."

We left that day.

July/August 1977

SPLIT

IN 1977 I DECIDED TO LEAVE MY MARRIAGE OF ELEVEN YEARS. Emotional loneliness and lack of intimacy had troubled me for most of my marriage. We lived separate lives and I felt I was dying inside. Yes, this decision was triggered by a peyote trip with my young lover, Larry, who had come into my life with his dark, dangerous Scorpio eyes and his drugs, seducing me into his dreamy occult world—about as far away from my suburban life as I could get. He fed me pills, pot, and hash. I opened my mouth and took relief from the pusher man to numb the pain of the affairs Vinny and I were each having.

That night I ate peyote and imagined I swam with the giant fish in the fish tank, leaving all perceptions of Larry's college dorm behind. What I learned from that fish convinced me I had to leave. "Fish don't fly in the sky," he said. "Birds don't swim in the ocean." I guess he didn't know about penguins, but I wasn't going to quibble. It was an "ah-ha" moment I couldn't deny.

I moved into the guest room that January, severing our marriage. A beautiful pine tree filled my window. I drew it over and over again. The sun sparkled through its snow-covered branches. As I stared, the tree seemed to dissolve into bright lights that danced before my eyes. I realized that nothing was solid, neither the tree nor me nor the vows we had taken.

What if I did leave? What if I took my children across the country camping?

VINNY WATCHED FROM THE HALLWAY AS I FILLED THE GUEST ROOM WITH African-patterned pillows, wicker baskets, and a secondhand Persian carpet, all for the new home I planned to make for myself and our kids. I had emerged from months of depression and grief that coincided with winter's snows and cold weather. Every morning I reached for the pen and paper by my bedside and wrote myself out of bed, expressing all the fears and unhappiness I had no one else to tell.

At four on the first morning of the July Fourth weekend, I closed the trunk of my red Opel station wagon after I had tucked my children, ages three and six, into their sleeping bags. Did Vinny look out the window at me, already foreign to him as I packed the car? Why didn't he say, "Don't go." If he had said it, would I have stayed? Was I too angry to be open to this? Behind the screen of my anger was the hurt little girl who wanted to be seen, invited in, told *Don't go.*

I was relieved to finally back out of the curved driveway, the house heavy with hushed silence. On a highway shoulder outside Philadelphia, I unfolded my map of the United States as the full moon shone in my window. Which way did I want to go? I had stashed six hundred dollars under the driver's seat along with a butcher knife and a half-ounce of pot. I told Vinny and my parents I was taking a vacation, but I was running away from home. My mother asked, "Are you taking the kids? Isn't that dangerous?," her face screwed up in a worried frown, her lips tight. Vinny offered no comment—neither stay nor go.

I shifted into gear and merged onto the nearly empty highway. *Who is my true family?,* I wondered as I drove into the night.

Eight years before, when Vinny and I had taken a similar trip to California in hopes of saving our marriage, I remembered a woman in a small sports car gassing up at a station between Las Vegas and Los Angeles. I leaned against our car, gulping cold water, watching her. *Someday I'll do that myself,* I thought. I imagined driving free and alone across the hot dry desert. I didn't imagine I'd have two children with me, but I had no other way to go and maybe I wanted them with me—a test drive for our new life: *Could we make it on the road alone?*

I surrendered to the unknown, I put myself in the center of what was alive and fierce inside me and let it grab the wheel and point me in a new direction. I drove through Ohio, down into beautiful green Kentucky and Tennessee. Past Memphis, the Mississippi cut across my path. Once I crossed it, like the Rubicon or the river Styx, there would be no going back. Late in the day, I drove onto the bridge and crossed the muddy waters shining with late afternoon sun. What I would find was that I had to be my own land, my own mighty river and exposed earth. I couldn't look to anyone to save me but myself. I crossed the Mississippi and drove into the gathering darkness.

Soon the forests turned into waving wheat fields. The first few days we stopped at state parks to have breakfast or lunch. I looked for lakes where we could swim and rest in the afternoon. After dinner I'd dress my kids for bed, kiss them goodnight, and tuck them in. I drove into the night, smoking marijuana until I ran out of steam. I'd find a rest stop, lock us in, and crawl into the back to sleep with my children.

By the end of the July Fourth weekend I coasted into the first rest stop in New Mexico, turned off the car and leaned over the steering wheel, exhausted. *I'm home,* I remember thinking as I looked at the dark desert that surrounded us.

The forests near Santa Fe and Taos were everything New York was not. Filled with wildflowers, rushing streams, clear vistas, and desert stripped clean of anything superfluous, they were a place of rest for my weary soul. The dust my car raised behind me erased the world as I knew it. The aspens surrounding our campsite provided all the music I needed as the wind gusted through their leaves.

My children seemed to go along without much complaint. Maybe the new sights and sounds fascinated them. Maybe I was raising two adventurers.

I didn't know anyone who would take a trip across America with two children under six and only a vague plan to reach the Pacific. Sometimes I was lonely and wanted to talk with a friend, or I found myself on a deserted road and wondered what the hell I was doing, but I kept going. I had a fantasy that on some road out West I would come upon a group of people waving for me to stop. "We've been waiting for you," they would say.

My mother was the only person I called, from a roadside phone booth outside Taos. "I'm fine," I said. Inside I wanted to say, *Mommy, I'm so far away from home, and I'm not coming back the way I was when I left.* I felt her worry and fear, but it came across as disapproval, which hardened me. What she really meant was, *Ginger, I'm afraid for you. Are you okay? What about my two beloved grandchildren, are you caring for them?*

I rounded a mountainous bend, where I don't remember, but what I do recall is the view. Wind blew up from the valley, bringing faint sounds—the echo of the wind—up to greet me. I stepped into another world, one with no buildings, roads, or towers, just the land as it always was, as tribes two hundred years ago would have seen it.

> *I felt I had dropped back into my body. Where had I been? I had been gone a long time, maybe my whole life, yet now I knew what being back felt like. The wind continued to flirt with me, blowing gusts and retreating. What made this vista so special was that it offered me a chance to see the earth unspoiled and to realize the pain of seeing it covered over with cities, junkyards, and oily rivers. As if my soul had also been despoiled and now, for the first time, I saw its purity, saw my original form mirrored in Nature.*

The wind washed over me; my children slept. I stood there for a long time—nowhere to go, no need to do anything but gaze across the land and let it enter me; I who had given up communion inside church walls years ago.

The earth was my mother, and I slept on her for a month. I slept deep, waking rested before dawn to the sound of the first birds.

We headed north for Colorado and Mesa Verde. I found a campsite late in the day, set up our tent and began making a fire. My children played at the picnic table as I shucked corn and basted chicken.

A man from the adjoining campsite sauntered over and introduced himself as Jack, saying, "My friend and I think you're very brave traveling alone with two children. When you get them asleep, please come over and join us for some wine." He seemed friendly. My New York antenna for weirdness was up, but I decided I liked him. Tall and lanky with black hair and an angular face, he reminded me of a pirate.

Later I walked between the rocks separating our campsites. Beside their picnic table was a powder blue Jeep. Jack busied himself stirring a pot of stew. The table was set with plates and wine glasses. The tailgate of the Jeep was down and I could see all kinds of food and liquor—a moving kitchen. Jack poured me a glass of wine. His partner backed out of the tent and said hello. Raymond was in his twenties, good looking with long curly blond hair. From his accent I knew he was British. He held a silver flute in his right hand.

Jack ladled out a bowl of Cajun stew. With the first spoonful, my eyes watered and my tongue was on fire. I wasn't used to spicy food. Raymond began playing his flute. Jack joined us and poured himself a glass of wine. Soon, a tall man from the campsite on the other side of Jack's came over and introduced himself as Dave.

We began trading stories. Dave lived near Syracuse, but was moving to Austin, Texas. Jack was a New Orleans native.

I told them I had to check on my children. I peeked into the tent. They were both curled up, sound asleep, so I went back.

Jack brought out a joint and we passed it around. I was surprised at how comfortable I felt with these three gay strangers. Wrapped in the firelight under a sky full of stars, swapping stories with my travel buddies, I no longer felt alone.

The next morning, while I fixed breakfast, Jack came over to tell me he and Raymond were going to Monument Valley with Dave. He asked if I wanted to meet them there, telling me they'd love to see me again.

I had to wash clothes and give my children baths. Then we were going to see the ruins. I told him I'd see how things went.

I turned this new idea over in my mind as I looked at the map and calculated the distance, about three hundred miles. Did I trust these men? What if they were leading me into a trap? Now I was thinking like a paranoid New Yorker, but that's how I'd learned to view the world and it probably kept me safe. *Do I want to shut down?*

By mid-afternoon we were back in the car driving through the Navaho Reservation.

I scanned the dry land, the organic way it undulated to the horizon, very different from the city. Small whiskers of dried grass and cactus peppered each hill. The openness of the sky frightened me. There seemed to be no boundaries except the far-off mesas and the wind rolling across thousands of miles of bare ground; a hundred million years of accumulated silence. Heat rose up from the black road, sweat poured down my face. I was alone in the vastness with my children asleep in the back, their faces red with heat, their wet hair etching the sides of their heads. I passed a dead animal, a cow maybe, its feet in the air. My dreams felt small and fragile. One harsh word would cause them to shatter and fall to the ground, vaporized in the hot sun. I held tight to the steering wheel as if it could hold me upright.

"Mommy?" came a sleepy voice from the backseat, "I'm hungry."

I didn't want to stop. I reached over to the passenger's seat, rummaged around in the cooler for bread, peanut butter, and jelly. Driving the straight desert road with my knees, I unscrewed the jar, made a sandwich, and passed it back to Jenny.

I drove a hundred miles before the turnoff to Monument Valley. I thought about Jack and Raymond. I felt accepted into their world, free from unwanted attention by men who wanted to fuck me. A great relief.

The sun had set by the time I saw the turnoff. Tall red sandstone mesas rose out of the desert like a fleet of ships floating in sand. The campsite road was treacherous and I knew from Long Island beaches that if I didn't take it fast, I'd mire in the sand. I backed up and gunned the engine. The speedometer hit seventy as we slammed through, spraying fans of sand to either side. Up ahead on the horizon I spied the powder blue Jeep and relaxed. They were here! I followed the road to the edge of the canyon. Jack, Raymond, and Dave yelled and crowded around me. We hugged like family at a reunion. I brought my kids out of the back and there were more greetings. Jack presented me with an extra dry martini on the rocks. He raised his eyebrow saying, "We travel in style."

I raised my glass and took a long gulp. The gin slid down my parched throat like a caress.

He motioned to the picnic table at the edge of the mesa, where dinner awaited. Our view took in the whole of Monument Valley. The wind whispered around the outcrops, the red-streaked sky was fading to muted tones.

After it grew dark, I prepared the children for bed, this time in the car. I reassured them I'd be sitting at the table nearby.

The moon rose as we passed around a joint. Jack suggested we sleep at the edge of the mesa. We agreed. The four of us lined up in a row, laughing as we wiggled into our sleeping bags. Looking up, all I could see were stars from horizon to horizon in the ink-black sky. Somehow, lying on the ground at the edge of the mesa with three men I'd just met yesterday didn't seem strange.

> *This was the first time I slept outside with no screen between the night and myself, not even the canvas tent walls that gave me the illusion of safety. My body felt alive to the night. Every cell was awake. The wind sighed across the valley like a voice I had come this far to hear. Blast me open, do your work. I've come for this, for what was beyond words or mind: the velvet sky, filled with more stars than I'd ever seen. And how dark it was! No city lights, no noise of millions of people. The quiet filled me, the stillness that was more alive than the sounds of traffic. I am here. I have always been here; I will always be here. I said yes to this. It was like nothing I had ever experienced before. Beyond the outer story of my journey, I had come for this.*

The last thing I remembered was a ceiling of stars that seemed to close around me, wrapping me up like a blanket. I could see the faint dark shapes of the mesas outlined against the sky. Such a big sky! The earth seemed small in comparison. The wind came in gentle gusts, lifting strands of my hair and brushing my face. With a great sense of peace, I relaxed into the earth and slept.

Wind and cold drops of rain woke me sometime in the night. I opened my eyes but saw no blanket of stars, only darkness. The wind blew hard and steady. I had to check on my children. They were awake and frightened when I opened the car door.

"Mommy, where were you? I'm scared. I was calling but you didn't answer," Jenny said.

I climbed into the back of the car and held them close. It was warm inside compared to the outside temperature. They snuggled into my body and went back to sleep.

The morning light was leaden gray and great roiling clouds poured across the darkened sky, the sun and warmth of yesterday gone. I stepped out into freezing temperatures, jarred awake. Wrapped in sweaters and jackets against the cold wind, we huddled with our three traveling companions around the table. There was no point in driving around, which disappointed me since I wanted to see the valley. We decided to move on to Grand Canyon.

By mid-afternoon I pulled into the general store at the North Rim. Jack's Jeep was already there. As I opened the back to help my kids out, Dave pulled into the space next to us.

We walked the aisles gathering food for dinner. Jack held three steaks and told me he was buying them for us. "I know money's tight," he said. I thanked him, unable to say more.

Before I could get our tent up at the campsite, Dave and Jack grabbed it. I went over to help, but they shooed me away. I leaned against a tree watching them, thought of myself lugging groceries home nine months pregnant. Vinny never asked if I needed help. Was I self-sufficient because of my nature or because I had no choice? Either way, it felt good to be taken care of. Jack started the grill and basted the steaks, freeing me from dinner responsibility. I played a game with my children. We were camped on a hill surrounded by tall pines. Dave came over and started talking with Jenny. She looked up at him, a big smile on her face.

This evening was the first time we'd set up camp and had hours to talk before dark. *This is what it must be like to have older brothers.* My own brother and I had grown closer since I decided to leave Vinny.

In the morning the men planned to hike into the canyon. I couldn't join them with my kids. After breakfast we said goodbye. Jack gave me his address and phone number. We hugged and he wished us a safe trip. I kissed and thanked them. The last I saw, they were hoisting packs on their backs.

I had asked who my true family was. Then in a remote campground, Jack, Raymond, and Dave gave me a new model for what men could be—compassionate and accepting. Although I had known them only three days, their caring gave me the strength to trust that what I needed would manifest in my life when I was ready.

I continued on, driving across mountain and desert, visiting national parks until we reached the Pacific. Stopped by the barrier of water—fluid, enormous, demanding, wild, I thought, *What now?* A storm was rising over the ocean, lightning crashed as I stood high on the Oregon cliffs. I was free like never before, but understood that I had to go home, face the end of my marriage, and move into my own life.

Irvington, NJ—1978

MUD

I held a Polaroid taken of Jenny, Jeremy, and me in 1977 after we came back from our cross-country trip and moved to Irvington, New Jersey. The three of us squeezed so close to the camera that we looked distorted. I studied their red cheeks, their open, expectant faces. Was this after the hospital, after I spun out of control? Their faces looked wary, as if they were thinking, *Can we trust Mom to be solid? Can we trust that she won't fall away again?*

I looked like I had screwed up my courage and we recorded the moment to prove it.

I wanted to leave them with Vinny because I didn't think I could raise them. I felt shaky and scared, maybe I couldn't rise to this. I remember Jenny coming down the hallway of our South Orange house after Vinny told her I was leaving. She stood in front of me and demanded, "Take me with you." She was six. I said yes. I didn't know how I would do it, only that I would.

After I left with the children, my life broke down. I could no longer keep up the cheery momentum or fantasy that everything would be okay in three months or that Vinny was my only problem.

I fell off the cliff of false safety my parents had given me, the false safety of not facing my emotions. They rose up ugly and demanding, and I couldn't stuff them back in. My former life cracked like dried mud and crumbled off me until I was naked and raw, unable to do anything but hallucinate and shake in fear. I shook down the foundation of the rotted house I stood in, shook with all my might until I hit the ground. The ground was solid, but I didn't see it then. I only saw that I was crazy. I'd released all my demons to parade before me and everyone else, and felt ashamed that I could no longer hold in the unacceptable emotions like my family had taught me.

What I didn't know then was that what I did saved me. The locked ward of a mental hospital didn't feel like a breakthrough, though. Instead, I felt myself sliding down a long dark passageway towards madness. At the bottom of the slide, a door waited. If I opened it, death would provide the blessed relief of letting it all go and jumping into oblivion.

My children saved me. I drew pictures of them in the hospital, knowing that somehow I must pull myself together enough to walk out, go home, and raise them. I loved them dearly. They held for me the love I couldn't hold for myself. In their innocent faces I saw the hope of a way out, that by loving them I could love myself. I took their hands and let them lead me back into life. And they so willingly took my hands that I was humbled and made right enough to pull myself out of hell.

BREAK

That final night in January 1978 before I took my kids to my parents and fell apart, I knew I was in deep trouble. I had kicked my boyfriend, Larry, out a week before and stopped taking drugs. I hadn't been able to sleep or eat much since. Jenny had been buying eggs, milk, and bread at the corner grocery, and making French toast for Jeremy and herself.

My mind wouldn't shut down. It battered me all week with recriminations, making me responsible for all the wrongs of the world. Without drugs to keep my feelings numbed, I realized how precarious my situation was—no job, two kids to raise alone in a sketchy neighborhood. I didn't know how we would survive and tried to come up with solutions, anything to keep me from losing my grip on the world. Nothing made any sense.

That last night, standing in the glare of the bathroom light, I surrendered to the chaos inside that I'd struggled hard to control.

Around midnight, I was convinced that we had to go west like we had done the previous summer. I gathered clothes, pillows, and blankets and stashed them in the trunk of my car. I filled plastic containers with food because we were evacuating. Escaping. I felt completely abandoned, unable to think clearly or reach for help. I paced the rooms while my children slept, sure that the world was coming to an end. I had to get them to a safe place—the west—before it did.

Around five, before the late January dawn, people emerged from their houses, walking silently in pairs towards the boulevard in Irvington, carrying brown paper bags. *Oh my God, they were leaving the planet!* I raced upstairs to wake my children. I didn't want them left behind. Sleepy-eyed, they stared at me as I hurried them to get dressed. Jenny asked, "Where are we going? It's the middle of the night."

"We have to go west."

I herded them into the car. We sat there shivering, waiting for the heater to kick on. *Which way should we go?* I asked myself. *Which road would get us away from here the fastest?* I turned on the lights; saw that the gas gauge was almost on empty. Rummaging through my pocketbook, I found three dollars, not enough to get us anywhere. I had quit my job as a typesetter two weeks earlier because I couldn't handle the stress. Now I needed money to go west.

Would the company take me back?

Holding my children's hands, I walked into my former office just as everyone arrived for the morning shift. I asked for my boss and after a muffled phone conversation, the receptionist sidled out the door. My boss came in and stared at me.

"Can I have my job back? Please. I need it."

He looked everywhere but straight at me. My reflection in the glass window behind him revealed to me how disheveled I looked. I hadn't showered in days. I wore the same clothes I had slept in for I didn't know how long.

He called for his son, who was my age, and I heard him whisper into the phone, "I can't handle her. She looks crazy. Would you deal with this?"

When his son arrived, he said, "You can't have your job back. We've hired someone to replace you. You'll have to leave." He talked to me as if I were a child or maybe a crazy person, all the while moving us towards the front door and out of their office.

Then Jenny spoke up. "Mommy, I have to go to school." I looked at her standing against the wall under the Jobs Pending board. *What was I doing here?*

I mumbled, "Let's go," and led the kids through the office, my head down, unable to meet the stares of my former co-workers.

I was in trouble but waited, shaking, in the kitchen until Jenny came home from school. Then I packed a bag and we drove to my parents' apartment in Bayonne.

The Garden State Parkway in late afternoon was crowded with early rush-hour traffic. I pulled up to the tollbooths at Newark Airport, shaking. The planes taking off and landing over our heads frightened me. They flew so low I thought they were aiming for us. I merged onto the New Jersey Turnpike and exited at Bayonne. My parents were waiting at the front door when we arrived. My phone call alerted them that something was wrong. They might not understand my problems, but at least my kids would be safe.

They already had dinner cooking. My kids moved into the comfortable routine they had at my parents'. I couldn't feel any comfort being there and paced the rooms, agitated. After dinner, my father insisted we stay the night and began opening up the sleeper couch in the living room. I knelt in front of the little table that held the latest jigsaw puzzle they were working on and searched the floor. When my father asked what I was doing, I told him I was looking for the missing pieces. My mother hurried to the kitchen. I heard her talking on the phone, first to my brother Jim and then to his wife Lynn, a nurse.

I viewed my surroundings as if I was encased inside a glass bubble. Voices came from far away. My parents tucked my kids into their own bed. I was unable to sleep and paced the living room floor. The streetlights shone in through the windows, casting harsh shadows. I heard planes flying into Newark. I needed to go into the city, take the tunnel to see a friend of mine, an astrologer. I repeated "exact change speeds trips," as if it were a mantra that, if said often enough, would calm me down and keep me steady. What I really felt was that I was slipping away. Terrified, I feared I would never return.

I understand that Carrier Clinic, where my brother and Lynn took me, provided a safe place to rest and find my way back, though what I remember most was how at night I panicked, unable to believe that the sun would rise again or that morning would come. I wrapped myself in a blanket and huddled by the nurses' station just to see another human. At first the doctors admitted me to the locked ward and prescribed Thorazine. After a few days I refused the pills. I played cards and smoked, with the TV running constantly. Other patients rocked in corners or talked to themselves, strapped into chairs. I asked what was wrong with me. No one had an answer. I found AA meetings with titles like "Anger," "Guilt," or "Fear." At last something made sense and I ended up in a twenty-eight-day drug rehab program. Every week I received drawings from my children and encouraging letters and cookies from my friend Maureen. After two months I realized I had to go home and raise my children.

I left Carrier Clinic in March 1978. Though officially spring, the weather was still cold and gray. My parents drove me to my brother's house to pick up my car. He had fixed it while I was in the hospital. Grateful for his help, I asked if we could stay with them. He hesitated, looked away, then said no. I didn't stay too long. I had a two-hour drive to Hempstead, Long Island, to pick up my children from Maureen and Jim's house. My father's health prevented my parents from taking care of my children, but my dear friends had come forward to take them while I was away, even though they had two children of their own under six.

"Mommy, Mommy." Jenny ran down the path to greet me. She grabbed my hand. "Look what we made for you." She led me to a poster taped to the front door that said "Welcome Home Mommy," surrounded by hearts, a bright yellow sun, and flowers. I knelt and hugged her. "That's beautiful." Jeremy peeked around the corner of the doorway. I walked over and kissed him. Maureen stood in the doorway of the kitchen, crying. I was too. Did she need any help? She shook her head. "Why don't you visit with the kids?"

Jenny talked about school. She was keeping up with first grade. Jeremy showed me his Tonka trucks, the ones he'd taken on our cross-country trip. Jim walked in with their children, Shannon and Sean. I hugged them, still feeling awkward. How could I thank them enough for taking my children and caring for them? They told me Vinny had only come once to visit the children in the seven weeks they had been there.

Maureen wanted me to stay. I wanted to buy food and go home. I was afraid that if I stayed with Maureen I would collapse into the comfort of her friendship and lose my determination. I knew what awaited me. I was scared. Could I do this?

Meeting Maureen and Jim—1970

PORCH

In 1970 Vinny and I were supposed to move to Maryland, but his new job fell through after he'd already quit the old one. We were on vacation in Maine, staying in a Bar Harbor bed and breakfast for one night. We had just come back from blueberry picking, or at least I was picking. Vinny stayed in the driver's seat as I jumped out and filled a huge pail with ripe berries.

When we returned to the bed and breakfast, I brought our cat Whiskey down to the porch while Vinny went upstairs.

That's when I met Jim. He came up the porch stairs and I offered him blueberries. He took a handful and we began talking. Whiskey had crawled under the porch, his leash stretched taut. Jim asked me who was under there.

I told him my cat's name was Whiskey. He didn't like to travel, but not being cat savvy, we hadn't figured that out.

Jim had an easy style. We talked about the geology book I was reading, then he told me he was on his honeymoon, his wife upstairs resting.

We said goodbye and after I pulled Whiskey from under the porch and went upstairs, I told Vinny about my encounter. He knocked on their door and invited them to dinner.

At dinner I met Jim's red-haired wife, Maureen, and we talked as if we were sisters. We feasted on food and drink, laughed until the waiters stacked the chairs and turned out the lights. When we returned to the B&B, we continued our conversation in the top floor hallway, laughing and talking until the owner shooed us to bed. We were making too much noise.

Maureen and Jim were headed to Nova Scotia and we were driving back to New Jersey the next day. We exchanged phone numbers and went to bed.

A pleasant evening with another couple, that's what we thought, but it was the start of so much more. The next month I became pregnant. Vinny called Jim, and we drove out to Hempstead, Long Island, for the first time. Soon this became the ritual. Every weekend either they drove to East Orange, New Jersey, or we went to Hempstead. Maureen and I spent every holiday together in the kitchen creating new and exotic dishes. The following year she became pregnant and we traded maternity and baby clothes. Two little girls, Jenny and Shannon, entered our lives. Soon two boys, first Jeremy, and then his best friend, Sean, arrived.

What made us pick that particular bed and breakfast in Bar Harbor? So much sprang from that porch. I still remember sitting on the rocker with a pail of blueberries cupped between my legs, popping their wild sweetness into my mouth as the warm sun lit up my book and the sharp pungent sea air filled my lungs, the gulls squawking and wheeling overhead.

I rocked and read, at rest. A new direction, at the time full of worry about jobs and money, opened before us—parenthood and the two children who would become my true family.

Irvington, NJ—1978

MOON

My kids slept in my car with our suitcases and the food we'd stopped to buy after leaving Maureen's. I opened the front door of my Irvington apartment. The living room was freezing. I'd run out of oil. No chance to order any until tomorrow. I left with snow piled high in the streets and now it was the first day of spring and the trees still dripped from the recent downpour. Dirty snowmelt ran in streams along the curb.

Our apartment was filled with the absence of life. Someone had taken down the Christmas tree and left stacks of presents heaped in the corner of the living room.

I wandered into the kitchen and opened the refrigerator, which I usually kept stocked with food. Even if I only had twenty dollars, I spent it on good food, a part of my Italian heritage. Empty. I could see the bare white walls, catsup, mustard, rice, and an old shriveled apple.

Vinny had told me he cleaned out the rotting food I'd gotten from the food co-op before I took my kids to my parents and not returned.

I walked the rooms like a disembodied ghost floating through someone else's life. Two months in Carrier Clinic had taken me to many places that bore no resemblance to my cozy living room with its rust-colored couch. My plants thrived. *Who was watering them?*

I descended the long flight of stairs and one by one carried my sleeping children up to my bed and tucked them under the covers, still in their coats. Then I brought up the bags of groceries and our clothes, a two-month accumulation I deposited inside the apartment door.

After I put the food away, I flipped on the bathroom light and stared at my tear-stained face in the mirror. I had cried all the way home while my children slept. I had no energy to think about any of it. I turned out the lights and crawled into the cocoon of my bed, already warm from their sleeping bodies. I snuggled down and reached across to draw them close. I smelled Jenny's newly-washed hair and felt the comfort of my own bed, surprised to find myself here after having gone so far away that I didn't think I could find my way back. I had no idea what I was supposed to do now.

THE FULL MOON ROSE ABOVE THE PROJECTS IN NEWARK ON THE OTHER side of the Garden State Parkway. During the day I was busy with my children, but now late at night, I felt like I had woken from a dream into an unfamiliar world. At times I thought I was trapped in the locked ward, yet nothing stopped me from going outside.

The early May breeze blew through the open kitchen window in small gusts, like breath. I shut off the light, brought a chair over, and leaned out, letting the sweet spring scent envelop me. Traffic whooshed by on the Garden State Parkway three blocks away, its steady hum floated over the rooftops. My children's newly washed socks and shorts flapped on the clothesline.

The wind blew from the east, carrying the smell of the highway, the restless moving metal, gas, cars never stopping. The buildings and trees loomed dark against the brilliant glitter of the moon. Its light turned the trees in the backyard into blue-grey shadows.

Was I the only one who stared into the night, unable to sleep? Restless thoughts jarred me awake night after night. I was alone and despite how shaky I felt, there was honesty about where I had landed. No pretense. No big house where I could pretend life was good. I was drawn to this working-class neighborhood due to lack of money, closer to my roots.

Years later I asked Jenny what she remembered about Irvington. Her memories were happy ones, which surprised me. Mine were about struggle, drugs, no money, fear, a nervous breakdown, and trying to make it through each day afraid the sun wouldn't come up in the morning. Here I confronted my emotions and my life. Here I searched for a new course, a way to create my own single life without a husband.

Jenny remembered her friends, the hammock they swung in, me throwing pots of cold water down from the second story kitchen window on hot summer days as they screamed with delight. She remembered the ice cream place, the corner store where she spent her allowance, school, Christmas, and decorating the tree.

I remembered staring at the traffic on the Garden State Parkway, wondering how I was going to take care of my children and how I would deal with the terror inside.

Irvington, NJ—1978

HAMMER

When I opened the door to my outpatient counselor's office the first time I returned to Carrier Clinic after my release, I didn't know whom to expect except that her name was Esther.

She walked across the room to greet us. I didn't have a babysitter that day so I brought Jeremy. She gathered up some toys and brought them over for him to play with while we talked.

I liked her right away. She seemed different from the therapists I'd met as an inpatient. Her voice was familiar, like so many I heard on the streets of New York. I looked around her office: plants hung from brackets at the window, a jar of seashells sat on the corner of her desk, and a poster from the Van Gogh show at the Met hung over the couch.

I wore a flowing purple Indian skirt, white blouse, and Frye boots. I watched her size me up as I took off my coat. She asked me how I was doing after my first week home.

I told her how scared I felt with the responsibility of taking care of my kids. I felt lost and overwhelmed. She reassured me that it took time to sort things out, but that I would get there. I eyed her suspiciously. Then she told me she'd come from a similar space. That surprised me; she looked so normal. I wanted to know what was wrong with me. None of the doctors in the clinic ever told me. She said I had a psychotic break brought on by drugs, most recently LSD.

I told her about Larry, how he always had drugs around because he sold them. But mostly I smoked pot, hash when it was available, sometimes took Quaaludes. I hated speed and coke. Drugs had helped numb the pain when my marriage went downhill, but I was through with them.

When I left, I took a deep breath, my steps on the stairs more solid. She didn't seem to think I was crazy. Maybe I could sort my way out of the tangle of my life.

After I returned from Carrier Clinic, my father visited me in Irvington. We sat down at the kitchen table and he reached into his pocket and handed me a check for a hundred dollars. I asked him what it was for. He jingled the change in his pocket, a lifelong habit he used to diffuse his feelings. He told me he would send me a hundred dollars a week until I settled my divorce.

I really needed the money. I had no idea how I was going to survive on the two hundred dollars a month Vinny gave me. My father helped me obtain a small disability settlement and I applied for food stamps.

I worked with Esther for a year until I decided to move from Irvington. My divorce from Vinny was final and I wanted to start fresh. I drove farther west in New Jersey looking for a small town, a suburban place with trees and affordable apartments. Although I wasn't more than thirty miles away, it felt like a foreign country. The same panic I experienced on my return from Carrier Clinic was back. Hadn't the year with Esther healed that? Again I felt shortness of breath, the ungrounded, queasy feeling in my stomach. The houses stared back at me. I didn't see many people. I was assaulted with loneliness and raced back to the noisy streets of Irvington. *Would I ever be able to move on?*

At our next session I told Esther I was crumbling inside.

She told me I needed to see her friend Roger in Manhattan and wrote his name and phone number on a piece of paper.

My mother called early in September—my father had been diagnosed with prostate problems. The day of his operation, I waited with my mother for the results. The surgeon told us they removed the cancer. That was the first time I heard the word "cancer"—maybe my ears refused to hear this before. At home I crawled numbly into bed. The next day I started crying and couldn't stop as the shock of my father's condition hit me.

WHAT A TUMULTUOUS FALL, WITH MY FATHER SICK AND MY MONEY FROM the sale of our home in South Orange running out. I had seventy-eight dollars in my bank account and the child support Vinny provided didn't cover my expenses. My therapist, Roger, urged me to look for work. I answered ads, but at first no one replied. One company seemed poised to hire me and then chose another candidate. A few weeks later, the employer called me—the person they hired hadn't worked out. Would I meet him at a local diner for a second interview? I must have convinced him I was qualified because he hired me.

I started the first week of December. I quickly recognized the huge gaps in my work experience, and hunkered down, watching the other two designers, scrambling to pick up enough skills to stay afloat.

After two months I began to feel more competent. I approached my boss and told him I noticed that the other designers had their own accounts, and I wanted my own too. He raised his eyebrows and said nothing as he sat behind his desk, tapping his fingers together. I had no idea what was coming. Maybe this hadn't been a good idea.

He informed me that he knew I had bullshitted my way into the job. Now I had the chutzpah to ask him for my own account. He shook his head, told me he was going to give me an account and not to ask him for any help, to figure it out myself.

I cried a lot that first year, frightened for my father whose health was getting worse. Many mornings I offered to buy coffee, so I could first go across the street to the Met Life building and find an empty phone booth. I closed the door and called Roger, my heart pounding. I had never shown anyone the depths of my fear and neediness, wanting to appear strong. Now I was raw. Could I trust Roger? I hated the job because I felt incompetent and was terrified of being fired. He listened to me sob, then reminded me that I needed to take care of my children. His soothing words reassured me enough to return.

DURING A VISIT TO MY PARENT'S APARTMENT IN BAYONNE AFTER MY father's cancer diagnosis, he motioned me into their bedroom, reached into the closet and pulled down a brown paper bag. I could tell from the way he hugged it to keep the contents from slipping out that it was heavy. He walked over to the bed and upended it. Out tumbled screwdrivers, rasps, a hammer, and enough tools for any job I might encounter—a gift to his daughter because he was leaving and wouldn't be able to fix things anymore.

I went to Home Depot and bought a toolbox. I lined up the screwdrivers and the pliers in neat rows and stacked the boxes of nails on the top shelf. I hefted the hammer in my hand, felt its weight, its no-nonsense job of driving nails to secure a window or fix a broken chair. The rough black rubber of the handle kept it secure in my grasp. I placed it gently on top of the other tools, closed the box, and latched it, thinking of all the broken things he fixed in my life using what few tools he had acquired from growing up in an orphanage.

As my father's cancer progressed, my mother reported on the many tears he shed, usually alone in the next room. Why was there no comfort, her arms around him? No matter, she had a hard time with emotions. I came near, perched beside my father, closer than I'd ever dared.

New Year's Eve 1979, I dropped my children off to attend a party in Manhattan.

Before I left, my father pointed to my new winter coat and said he was glad I'd finally be warm.

I glanced down at the pea green coat—its curls tight like a poodle. His words were warm, saying, *I'm glad you're taking care of yourself.*

I went into Manhattan in my turquoise silk blouse and raw silk pants—my favorite color—feeling beautiful. I don't remember the party except after it was over, laying in bed with the party-thrower, a middle-aged man, director of some horror movie filled with blood, gore, and violence. I wasn't present. I guess that's why I can't remember much, certainly not passion, certainly not being held or cherished. Only leaving quietly before dawn, picking up my clothes on a pretext of going to the bathroom, and getting the hell out of there.

I drove across the Verrazano Bridge into Staten Island on my way to Bayonne and took the first exit, searching for the ocean. I found a small sad beach strewn with trash. The first rays of sunlight rose over the ocean and lit the beach; shells and garbage crackled under my feet. I wrapped my coat tight against the cold; my turquoise pants flapped in the wind. I breathed the salt air. I had time to waste before reentering my parents' apartment where my father would ask how the party was and I would have to lie.

LUNCH

I wish I could remember the words my father and I spoke when we finally did get close, at my therapist Roger's urging, before he died in 1981. They've receded although the feeling hasn't—the way he waited to hear what I had to say when I invited him to lunch. The way we slowed down and carefully chose our words. His tentative smile, my hand reaching across the table to take his. The way I listened as he explained how his life was like a series of tidal waves crashing over him.

He was my father, but also a fellow traveler, doing his best while the cancer ate his body, sapping his strength.

I introduced an idea—it's not too late to love, to reach for the communication we failed to have all those years. We were still alive and best of all, willing.

Our hamburgers and fries grew cold, the waitress refilled our coffee cups and we talked on. We broke bread together. This was my father whom I had not known until then.

He asked me questions no one else ever had. After the many times I watched his head rise step by step from the subway after his twice daily two-hour commute, I asked, "What was your life like?"

And I set him straight. No, I was fiercely independent because I had to be. No one was there to protect me from his anger so I learned to fight.

He nodded.

What I had dreamed of was this—that we would look into each other's eyes as we told the truth.

Queens Village, NY—1984

RUPTURE

Two weeks before Christmas 1984 when Jeremy was ten, he woke with a stomachache. He wasn't faking so I stayed home from work. By late morning his pain had increased. I called the doctor. After I explained his symptoms, he told me to bring him in right away. I thought, *Oh boy, something is really wrong.* Jeremy couldn't bend over to tie his shoes so I helped him. I could see he was scared. I was too.

After examining him, the doctor told me that his appendix was about to rupture; I needed to drive him to North Shore University Hospital immediately.

After surgery, it was hard to see my son hooked up to an IV in the recovery room. His eyes fluttered open. I told him he was going to be okay. I had just spoken to the doctor.

He nodded, still out of it. I took his small warm hand in mine.

For the next week I stayed in the hospital with Jeremy. The nurses set up a cot for me next to his bed. After coming to see Jeremy the first day, Vinny left on a business trip. Six days later he showed up at the hospital.

The room was filled with our visitors and the ones visiting the boy in the other bed. My mother brought Jenny from home. She sat on the little cot I slept on since the day he was admitted. We talked about school and what she was doing while I was at the hospital. My life had shrunk down to the hospital room with occasional visits home. Jeremy sat in bed playing with his Legos on the blanket. He was eating the spaghetti and meatballs my mother brought—his Italian comfort food.

Seeing Vinny, I was hardly able to disguise my anger. My mother got up from her seat so he could sit next to the bed. He hugged Jeremy. "How are you doing, big guy?"

Jeremy shrugged his shoulders, said his stitches hurt. Our side of the room was silent, which made the laughter and banter from the other side seem louder.

I watched Jeremy finish his lunch as his father talked with him.

"Don't rush getting up," Vinny said. "You need to heal."

I interjected that he was walking every day. The nurses told us that walking would help him grow stronger. Ignoring me, Vinny repeated his words.

The nurse came in to get Jeremy ready to walk. He slid his feet off the bed. I put his slippers on, but with one foot on the floor, he started yelling, "Ouch, ouch, it hurts!"

I asked what was the matter. Again he cried out in pain.

"Jeremy, if you're in pain, you don't have to walk." Vinny turned to me, "Don't push him."

I wanted to spit at him. He hadn't been here the last six days, and now he sounded as if he was the authority on what to do. Jeremy was leaving the hospital on Tuesday and the doctor wanted to make sure he was healed before they released him.

Vinny ignored me and told Jeremy again to not overdo it, as if he could squeeze six days of caring into the tone of his voice.

The nurse stood beside Jeremy. I realized he needed his father's attention and with his "ouches" he was getting it.

Finally I said, "Enough. It's time to walk. I know it hurts but you need to do this if you want to get better." I helped him up, put in the position of being the bad guy. What the hell. Jeremy had improved every day before his father showed up. He was scared and needed reassurance. Nothing in his ten years had prepared him for a rush to the hospital doubled over in pain with me white-knuckling the steering wheel, racing from the doctor's office straight to the emergency room.

Jeremy took a few slow steps while we encouraged him. He gathered strength as he did first one circuit and then another of the room. I brought him his bathrobe and Vinny helped him slip his left arm in. I reached down to tie the belt.

Jeremy walked with the nurse's arm around his shoulders. She guided him out of the room into the white corridor. We watched him shuffle along. Soon he'd leave the hospital and return home with a scar on his belly. It would shrink and fade as his body grew. Yet what did he learn from his father? That a business trip was more important than being with his son? As I watched him move tentatively down the corridor, I wondered what else he would learn from this.

I thought back to the time after I came home from Carrier Clinic, when our life had felt tenuous and I counted on the two hundred dollars a month I received from Vinny.

He brought the children home after his weekend with them and turned to leave. I asked if he had my child support check, trying not to let my anxiety show.

He reached into his pocket saying he'd forgotten and pulled out the check. I hated being in the position of having to ask. I hated this power play. Sometimes the check bounced. Other times I asked and he told me he didn't have it and I'd have to wait.

Finally my anger overcame my fear. The next time he played the check game, I arrived at his Manhattan office dressed in my sexiest outfit and sashayed to his corner office.

He looked up from his desk, surprised to see me. I walked in, leaned my hands on his desk and looked him hard in the eye. "I'm done. If you don't pay child support on time, I'll take you to court. Now where's my check?" I spoke in a voice that carried to every corner of the office. People picked their heads up, leaned out of their cubicles listening to what was going on in their boss's office.

"You can't come in here and make demands like this."

"Oh, no? I'll let the courts decide. I've already talked to them."

He never gave me a late check again.

WHEN JEREMY CAME HOME FROM NORTH SHORE HOSPITAL AFTER HIS appendix was removed, we bought a real Christmas tree. That year we smelled fresh pine—a big difference from the hand-me-down fake tree. After Christmas I removed the decorations and carried the tree to the curb. When I came inside, Jeremy was crying. I asked what was wrong.

He was upset because I'd thrown the tree away. I told him that was what we did with Christmas trees when they dried out, but he wasn't satisfied and told me that nobody wanted him either. He was going to be thrown away too.

I told him that wasn't true and that I loved him.

He insisted that he wasn't special. I hugged him and told him he was. Then I suggested we write a letter to the tree explaining how much we loved it and how happy it made us. I brought crayons and paper, he drew a Christmas tree, and we wrote the letter. We went outside and taped it to the tree.

I could see this made him feel better. However, I could feel how Jeremy didn't trust his body after his appendectomy, as if it might betray him again. At first I thought he would overcome it, but realized he needed help to deal with this trauma—more than I was capable of giving him.

He didn't want to be in therapy. I dragged him the first day because I was clear he needed help.

The psychologist's report said he had a great fear of dying. Because we moved suddenly, leaving his father behind, and I was gone during my breakdown, he was afraid I would die and he would be abandoned. He was afraid of his own anger and suppressed it behind a façade of compliance. When upsetting events happened, such as an operation or poor school performance, he became frustrated or anxious and didn't know how to deal with it. His defenses were strong and enabled him to function surprisingly well. Care was needed to get past the defenses he had carefully erected. Helping him express his anger and fears would empower him.

When Jeremy, at four and a half, came to me on Halloween saying, I'm going to die, I saw the fear in his face. Did the skeleton and monster costumes scare him? I knew King Kong did. Focused on the ending of my marriage, I wasn't always very sensitive to his fears and regretted that.

We were in the orange kitchen in Irvington in 1978, the fall after I came back from Carrier Clinic. Maybe he thought he would die if I didn't come back to care for him. Clothes flapped on the line outside; it was late afternoon. I squatted down to reassure him that he wasn't going to die, not for a very long time. His face relaxed and I was the all-powerful protecting mother.

Did he have a premonition that "a very long time" would be fifteen years later?

See, There He Is

Bayside, New York—1990

CEASE

My mother died in April 1990 after a long struggle with Parkinson's disease. My father had died in 1981. Now I felt like an orphan. My brother, Jim, didn't come to our mother's funeral. I didn't understand why. I thought that when Mom died, we would draw closer. Instead, I lost the rest of my family—Jim, his wife, Lynn, and their two daughters. I was a tree uprooted and shaky.

When I talked to Jim on the phone about our mother's funeral, he told me that they had said goodbye to her at the nursing home in Fort Collins, Colorado, where she lived the last few years.

He wasn't sure they would be able to come back to New Jersey for her funeral. When I called again, he told me he wasn't coming because his horse was giving birth. I screamed that his fucking horses were more important than his mother's funeral. He hung up. I doubled over as if he had shoved a knife into my gut, shocked that my brother would abandon me to face our mother's funeral alone.

Jeremy walked into the kitchen, put his arms around me, and held me. He didn't say a word.

The day of my mother's funeral, he donned a suit and stood tall at the door, the man in the family, greeting the mourners who came to pay their respects to his Nanny. She was to be buried next to Poppy in New Jersey.

After my mother's death, my brother and I ceased communication. Too many emotions that we had never expressed came between us, and we, like two ice floes, drifted further apart in the frigid world that had become our connection. We didn't call across the void or question what had happened.

We went our separate ways, already two thousand miles apart. Sometimes I almost forgot I had a brother except that my heart ached. Even that hurt was covered over by a hard shell of anger that I wasn't ready to break. Holidays passed with no cards or calls. His two daughters grew and I only remembered Carol at eight and Melissa as a four-year-old with fine flaxen hair.

My cousin Florence asked about Jim. I shrugged my shoulders. She wanted me to reach out, but Jim had left New York years before, putting us all behind him as he recreated himself as a Colorado patent attorney and horse breeder.

Who had he become? I didn't know where to reach to open the door locked between us.

EVERY NIGHT AFTER MY MOTHER'S DEATH, I DESCENDED TO THE GARAGE, backed the car out into the driveway, and then turned on the light. I painted on paper cut into pieces with a razor and tacked together. All my rage and grief bled out through my fingertips. I painted abstract gestures, letting the paint speak what I couldn't. I created some of the drawings on my hands and knees, my fingers black from charcoal. I excavated, digging up primal emotions. A baby bird emerged from the swirling lines, its beak in profile. I drew feathers on its small wing. Its head hung down; a spiraling umbilical cord looped off the bottom of the paper.

DREAMS

— I gave birth to a two-year-old girl child. She asked if I was going to put her aside and only call for her when it was convenient.

— The two-year-old child and I crossed a night-dark sea on a thin board. I was afraid I couldn't get her safely across to the other side, yet I did.

— A group of wildflowers greeted me, yelling and screaming.

I THOUGHT OF MY FATHER PICKING BLACK-EYED SUSANS AND TIGER LILIES for me as a child on our many drives into the country. I listened to the messages coming through my dreams, listened to the voices in my head. I realized they were my parents' voices still criticizing me. Even though they were dead, and I had made peace with my father years ago, I kept the old destructive patterns alive within me.

Bayside, New York—1991

HIT

Now that Jeremy was healing from his first brain surgery, I wondered how I could help him. Questions troubled me. *What caused his cancer? How much did attitude have to do with his healing? What about unconscious factors?* His early childhood had been chaotic and I asked myself if that played a part in his experience of the world.

A few days later I went into his room and sat next to him as he lay on his bed watching TV. I asked him to turn the TV off because I had something I wanted to talk to him about.

At first he seemed not sure what was coming next. I asked if he remembered that I was in Carrier Clinic when he was three. He looked confused, shook his head no.

I was surprised that he had no memory of what, to me, was a huge trauma in my life. I told him I had a nervous breakdown and was in a hospital for two months. I wanted him to know in case he had feelings about my being gone. I didn't want scary memories locked inside him. I explained that I had a hard time when his father and I split and I took drugs from Larry. Did he remember him?

Jeremy didn't like him. That much was clear.

Neither did his sister. I told him that Larry lived with us for three months after we moved to Irvington. Then I asked him to leave. That's when I went to the hospital.

He was quiet, seemed to be taking in my words. I waited, my gaze drifting to the shelf above his dresser that held one of his old yellow Tonka trucks from that long-ago time.

"Nobody ever talked about it," he said.

"Did you know that I hit you when I got frustrated with you?"

Now he looked at me in surprise. "You did? But I'm such a nice person, why would you do that?"

"Because I was barely holding on and sometimes you wouldn't let up. It's no excuse. I learned later how to handle my frustration better. I'm sorry."

He didn't say much but at least I brought into the open some of my earlier regretted actions. I hoped that somehow this helped him.

I worried that somehow I had contributed to Jeremy's illness—bad food, the upheaval when he was very young, or the time I hit him.

LIP

When I came home from Carrier Clinic in 1978, I had trouble controlling my panic. I struggled to hold on and not be overwhelmed. Fear drained my strength and each decision seemed insurmountable. Especially at these times, because he was tuned into me, Jeremy demanded my attention by repeating a singsong phrase over and over, such as "Mommy, I want…" No matter what I said, he wouldn't stop. Like Chinese water torture, it addled my brain.

One such morning when he was four, I remember with a cringe. He ate breakfast at the kitchen table in Irvington, kicking his heels against the chair legs, still dressed in his pajamas. "No, you can't have it." This went on and on. I wanted to push him back where he belonged—the obedient child. Without warning I hauled back and hit him in the back of his head. He pitched forward and hit the edge of the table. His lip started to bleed. I immediately felt remorse. "Oh Jeremy, I'm sorry," I said, reaching for a napkin to staunch the blood. I grabbed ice cubes from the freezer, wrapped them in a towel and pressed them to his swollen lip.

I didn't hit him again after that. When his insistent demands grew too much, I locked myself in my room, called the parent abuse hotline and talked with them until I calmed down.

As I grew stronger inside with help from my therapist Roger, I gradually learned to handle my emotions. Jeremy just wanted comfort;

he just wanted me to pay attention to him; he just wanted me to connect and not drift away, he just wanted, and wanted...

...what we all want, to be loved and held and told it would be alright—a place of safety in his upheaved world.

Now I wonder if I caused the assault on his head to take hold.

I knew how serious his cancer was, stage 4. "An ugly tumor," Doctor Walker had said. I read the articles the doctor gave me: his life expectancy was two years.

We would be different. Somehow I'd find a way.

Bayside, NY—1991

DRILL

Jeremy's second operation was scheduled right before Thanksgiving 1991. I stayed with him the night before the radiation seed implants. Vinny didn't think it was necessary to be with him during this procedure. I didn't understand. *Was he insensitive or just not dealing with his emotions? How could I leave Jeremy to face this alone?*

They gave Jeremy a bed in the emergency room with curtains for privacy. I tried to make him comfortable, bringing water, cookies and a snack, yet the familiar hospital smells remained. I was too anxious to sleep in the uncomfortable chair and waited for what was to come. I checked on him. He was asleep.

The next morning the doctors arrived in Jeremy's room, brisk and businesslike. They brandished a drill, which they would use to make the holes for the metal halo. They sat Jeremy down and swabbed his head.

"Wait a minute," I said. "Aren't you going to give him anesthesia?"

They turned and looked at me. "Hasn't he had a shot?" one of them asked.

"No," I said. "And you're not going to touch him until he does."

Jeremy didn't say anything. Every cell in my body screamed, *What if I hadn't been there?*

They picked up their tools and left. Soon a nurse came in to give him a shot. He relaxed, slumping in his chair.

When the doctors returned, they pulled out the drill.

Jeremy was groggy. "Ma," he said, "you don't have to stay."

"I'm not going anywhere." I knelt before him and held his hands in mine. I watched them drill holes in Jeremy's head. I watched the blood flow down his face. I watched, intent on protecting him, which was an illusion.

I watched as they screwed a metal halo into his head to help align the radiation seeds they would implant during surgery. I walked with him to the door of the surgery room, holding his hand through the bars of the gurney. As they began to wheel him in, I bent down and kissed him. "*Vaya con Dios,*" I whispered in his ear. I stood there alone, as the door swung shut.

This was the third time I walked Jeremy to the swinging doors of an operating suite. These doors had a square window in them. Through them I watched the doctors push the gurney and turn left into the operating room. Once more I wondered if my son would be coming back.

I was waiting in his room when they brought him up from surgery. To protect visitors and the hospital staff, he wore a lead cap to keep the radiation from harming us.

Such a strange hat. Heavy, like a metal bowl overturned on his head.

He wore it for a week until the doctors removed the implants and he came home for Thanksgiving.

I was so focused on Jeremy that Jenny was thrown into the background as I talked to doctors, visited Sloan, and cared for Jeremy. She wasn't sure what was happening day to day. She told me she didn't feel part of the family, didn't feel in the loop. One day when I came home, I found her on the steps hunched over with her coat wrapped tight against the cold. She'd lost her keys and sat for hours waiting for me to get home. I unlocked the door and we went upstairs. I was with Jeremy at Sloan. Had she known, she would have come with me. I was so busy with Jeremy, I didn't think to ask her.

In the past, my life had frequently seemed like a series of frustrations and struggles, and I found it hard to move forward with ease. Now I felt like the floodgates had opened, and I was moving fast—in horror. Jammed awake, as if a loud noise had jarred me out of the dream state. I was disoriented, confused, and on edge. Wake up, wake up!! I existed in constant crisis mode, trying to make sense of the senseless. This was an altered state I didn't want to be in. When I moved past the shock, I drove around screaming. Praying to God for help. Anything. On my lunch hour I walked the woods along the North Shore of Long Island praying to the Earth, *Mother heal him, Mother help me.*

One day as I drove the Merritt Parkway in Connecticut going home from a press check at a printing company, Peter Gabriel's song, "Don't Give Up," played on the radio. My defenses cracked and the pain I felt at what was happening to Jeremy overwhelmed me. I couldn't see the road ahead through my tears and pulled into the next rest stop.

A woman in a drab raincoat knocked at my car window, drawn by the screaming inside. I heard her knock, most unusual for anyone to seek out a deranged person at the driver's wheel. I opened the door, sobbing. When I stood up, I looked down at the top of her white head.

She asked, "Are you alright?"

Fearless woman.

I shook my head no, screamed at her, "My son has brain cancer."

Without hesitation, she folded me into her arms and held me as I sobbed into her shoulder.

"Something told me I needed to pull in at this rest stop," she said. "Now I know why."

I looked at her and cried over and over, "God sent you to me!"

She told me she had lost her dear husband and knew what I was going through. "You are so young and pretty," she said. I felt neither. Now she was happy, having married again. Life had gone on even when she felt it wouldn't.

After all the years, I still remember her name—Pat Fitzgerald. Such a brief encounter yet I felt I was being watched over and that our lives and our struggle were not meaningless, that maybe, just maybe, some larger force—God—cared.

Bayside, NY—1991

POND

JEREMY WAS SCHEDULED TO HAVE HIS FIRST CHEMO TREATMENT RIGHT before Christmas 1991. On Christmas morning, instead of opening his presents as he had done every year with his sister, he was vomiting. I brought him water and sat next to him on his bed. Outside his window, a gray morning loomed without a break in the clouds, not even snow that would have made it festive. Nothing felt festive. I reached around and handed him the stuffed pink pig that had been attached to get-well balloons. He punched it. Neither of us said a word.

THAT WINTER I NEEDED TO DO SOMETHING PHYSICAL TO DISCHARGE some of my stress. I thought of the pool at my health club but discovered it was closed for the season.

What now? I could walk around the duck pond down the hill even though it was cold and miserable. I dressed warmly and took off, not expecting much.

Should I take the left path or the right path? I took the right and began walking. It was cold, yet I wasn't alone. A few hardy early morning walkers circled the pond. I looked at the ducks, geese, and wild birds. Their sounds soothed me. I was in my own world; nothing could reach me here. Tension washed out of me. Even in the dead of winter life continued. The ducks slept on the ice, flew around, pecked at each other.

As I walked around the duck pond in the early mornings, gathering courage to face the day, I noticed the birds that lived there—Canada geese, the swan couple, and different ducks all swam up for food. Soon I came to know which ducks hung out together. Later I watched the swans build their nest in the reeds.

The pond became my haven where I could release stress and connect to nature. After the baby swans were born, their parents took them for a swim, father leading, mother in the rear, with six gray fuzzy chicks in between. Flocks of red-winged blackbirds flew through the trees. One rainy morning I came upon a great blue heron perched in a tree overlooking the lake.

I realized that we needed a home close to nature instead of the noise, dirt, and congestion of the neighborhood we lived in. The rent in Bayside had gotten too high and with Jenny moving into Manhattan in June when she turned twenty-one, I could no longer afford it. I wasn't sure where to start looking.

At first I searched Queens, driving around neighborhoods near Long Island Sound. The houses were rundown and the neighborhoods didn't attract me. Jeremy wanted to live in a house, and I was determined to find one.

I turned to Nassau, the first county outside New York City limits. A Realtor drove me around Glen Cove but again saw places I wouldn't bring my son to.

After leaving the last depressing dump, I lost my way and drove up a hill into a town I'd never seen before. The sign said, "Welcome to Sea Cliff." The well-kept houses were set back on tree-lined streets, more like what I had in mind.

The more I drove around, the more I knew I had found home. The roads wound around the hills through quiet streets, all of them leading down to Long Island Sound. Waves lapped at a little beach. The town center was one long quaint block with a few antique stores. I parked my car and walked around. Old Victorian houses painted bright colors dazzled me. I found a real estate agency called Harmonious Homes and took down its number.

The second house the Realtor showed me cost more than I could afford, but a woman healer lived there part time and paid a share of the rent. As we drove up the driveway to the Victorian cottage, I said to myself, *You mean I could actually live here? I could actually have this?*

High bushes and trees surrounded the corner property, which was secluded though in the middle of town. A beautiful weeping cherry tree swooped down over the front steps, which led to a porch that wrapped around two sides of the house. The living room had a fireplace. I stopped seeing the details after that. I met Puja, the woman healer, in between her sessions and she seemed pleasant. The owner and I hit it off. I heard myself say that I wanted to leave a deposit to rent the house. I drove back to work thinking, *Are you crazy? You just rented a house with a woman you don't know. Maybe she's into weird cults.* Another part of me, the part that had taken control and moved effortlessly in these new directions, said, *Relax, we're doing this.*

What I see now is that this "crazy" part of me was my intuition, the inner guidance that I hadn't come to trust yet. As time went on, I began to rely on these impulses. Fear still came up when I faced an unknown situation. My parents taught me as a child to stay safe, but I discovered that was not how I wanted to live. I began to choose growth instead of safety.

When I thought of the two women in the house, both white-haired, I remembered the dream I had a year earlier: *I was attempting to climb steep cliffs that dropped off into the sea. The waves below broke on the rocks with a sucking noise. The cliffs were unsteady, made of Styrofoam. I kept slipping down toward the rocks and the pounding surf.*

Somehow I crawled to the top where two white-haired women pulled me up and took me to their cottage.

Now, here were those white-haired women again.

Bayside, New York—1992

WINGS

In September 1991, when Jeremy was a senior at Benjamin Cardozo High School in Bayside, his life spread open like wings. We sent letters to colleges, talked of where he wanted to go and what he might major in. Would he stay at home or go away? He joined the yearbook staff. It was all too brief. In the chaos that descended on us in October, I hardly remembered how much pleasure it gave me to see him open up and grow.

After his diagnosis, I was determined to keep him in school so he could finish senior year with his class. Despite the radiation treatments and the chemotherapy, he completed high school and the following June graduated with his class.

Jenny, Vinny, Kyle, and I watched as the long line of blue-gowned seniors snaked their way towards the dais to receive their diplomas. "Is that him?" we asked and pointed to different students. Then we saw him as he climbed the stairs and walked across the stage. "See, there he is!" I yelled and grabbed Jenny's arm as Kyle took pictures. Vinny beamed. I heard them call out, "Jeremy Cahill," and my eyes filled with tears. When everyone was back in their seats, on cue, they flung their caps in the air. I watched Jeremy fumble to get his baseball cap out of his pocket to cover the bald spot and put it on his head before tossing his mortarboard high into the air.

LOUDSPEAKER

Before Jeremy got sick, I pushed him to get a job because he wanted to learn how to drive. I told him I would teach him on my old Toyota, but he didn't want to learn on a stick shift. His school offered lessons, and he wanted me to pay. I said no. He whined. Complained. Hounded me. I said, "If you want to take lessons, get a job and I'll pay for half. Show me you want it bad enough and I'll help you. Get off your ass and do something." He bitched and moaned, but I stood firm.

It took him months to find a job. I saw he was scared. I drove him to fill out applications and waited in the car. His friend worked at Waldbaum's supermarket. At first Jeremy wasn't interested, but one day he told me Waldbaum's hired him to stock shelves. For the first time, he made his own money. He began saving for a car.

When he worked late, I picked him up. From outside I watched him and his friends laugh as they stocked shelves. The store was closed. Radios blared from the aisles. They drank soda and ate cookies while slapping prices on cans and boxes.

I walked up to the window and tapped to get Jeremy's attention. When they saw me, one of the boys got on the loudspeaker and announced, "Jeremy, your Mommy's here to pick you up." After more laughter, he came out front hissing, "Wait in the car."

RIGHT BEFORE JEREMY'S GRADUATION, JENNY FOUND AN APARTMENT ON 82nd Street in Manhattan. This time she was ready to move out on her own. She had a steady job with a high-end wall-covering company and although I wanted her to finish high school, I was proud that she was making her way in the world. She started out as their receptionist and had been promoted to customer service. She developed a rapport with the customers and her warm friendly personality enabled her to collect overdue payments. Her bosses saw she was an asset to the company.

I gave her money for a new daybed and other moving expenses and told Jeremy I would help him buy a car. He was accepted into St. John's University and would need to drive from our new home in Sea Cliff to Queens every day.

On moving day, Jeremy and I drove into the city to help Jenny. A few of her friends showed up and we unpacked boxes. The day was hot so we opened the French doors, hoping for a breeze. The streets overflowed with Saturday shoppers and strolling families. We ordered pizza from the corner restaurant and sat around on the floor eating our slices. Jeremy and I left Jenny that evening and drove back to Bayside to finish our packing. We moved in two weeks.

Sea Cliff—1992

HAVEN

An invisible thread connects me to the town high on the cliffs where I still walk in my imagination down the hills and past the bright Victorian houses, to the water that flows in and out of Hempstead Harbor twice a day, bringing in fresh water and returning what is old to the sea.

My world changed the first time I drove Sea Cliff Avenue, past the sycamore trees lining the road that wound around the harbor and up the hill into town. I needed to be outside the everyday world, perched on the cliffs, watching the planes come into La Guardia Airport, tiny and far away, unable to touch me here.

The bay was deep and dark, as was my life back then. The wind blew across the cliffs, howling and tossing the trees. Way below, Long Island Sound led to the sea. The bay I walked beside was scoured out ten thousand years ago by the glacier that formed the land this town rests upon. I walked in all kinds of weather, even blizzards, and watched the snow erase the rest of the world. Oh how I wished it would! How I wished it would erase me too! But the cliffs were solid. The streets, like the veins of my heart, led me back to my home every night, back to the quiet. How quiet and how much I loved it. Who knew I would love the quiet where I never felt alone?

My life ended there and then began again. I was surprised to feel the town's soul embrace me. I rested against its heart like a child protected within the womb.

THE COTTAGE I RENTED, ALTHOUGH BEAUTIFUL, NEEDED UPDATING. I requested a two-year lease, knowing we needed a safe peaceful haven. It was everything the attached garden apartment in Bayside wasn't—cool and shaded in the middle of town. Tall windows let in filtered light.

The rooms were decorated in odd color combinations—maroon with bright orange paisley wallpaper. The owner was an interior designer—for whom I couldn't imagine.

I never lived with anyone but family before sharing the house with Puja. She occupied the largest room down the hall from my bedroom. We shared the kitchen and bathroom.

When I took Jenny and Jeremy to see it, I got mixed reactions. Jeremy hated it. Jenny loved it. She said to Jeremy, "It's time for Mom to have her own life. She's been raising us for twenty years and now it's her turn. You're going to be leaving home, just like I am. She's been giving to us, moving for us, and now it's time for her to move into a place she loves." I was surprised to hear her words and felt tremendously cared about and supported. I had mixed feelings about this move because I knew Jeremy didn't like the cottage. He'd already had too many unwanted changes.

Did he fear that this would be the last house he would live in?

A winding staircase led to his attic room. Across the hall was a storeroom filled with junk, its doorway covered by old Indian-print fabric.

Jeremy actually had two rooms: a sitting area with his desk and dresser and a bedroom with a skylight above the bed. I envisioned all kinds of possibilities.

I dragged up two quarts of white paint to cover the maroon walls. I laid carpet and cut extra squares, piecing them together like a jigsaw puzzle. It was the best I could do. Initially his mattress was on the floor because we couldn't move his captain's bed up the stairs. Later I hired two men to remove the window and haul the bed up with pulleys.

The first morning, I woke at seven to footsteps on the porch outside my window. Wondering who it could be, I peered out from behind the curtain at Puja's first client.

Puja was here to work and other than during her quick forays into the kitchen for containers of food, I saw little of her until after nine that night. She was cheerful as we chatted over tea.

I watched her, every day the same upbeat energy. I'd never known anyone like her. I seemed to know moody, volatile, sad, or depressed people. She was different and I was intrigued. "What exactly is an energy healer?" I asked her.

Sea Cliff felt different from any other place I'd lived. The homes looked cherished, the gardens tended. Summer flowers and trees bloomed in every yard. Wind chimes tinkled in the breeze on porches decorated with comfortable furniture for entertaining friends or relaxing with a good book. This healing energy felt like the energy of the duck pond. When Jeremy and I moved to Sea Cliff, I wanted to heal myself as well as him.

If I could plant a garden in Bayside, rather than wait for some mythical future in which to have one, then I could start to feed the starved parts of my soul. If I could walk around that duck pond every day and let nature heal me, then I could no longer live in a place that was harsh and stressful. The garden led to the duck pond, led to Sea Cliff, led to my new life. Each step seemed small until I turned around and saw the path of footprints behind me.

In Sea Cliff I walked around town rather than around the duck pond. I walked midnight streets soaking in peace through my pores, into my cells. I released the transience of the city, the rushing people. I replaced it with streets lined with ancient trees; the wind rustling their leaves soothed me as I walked. Crows, cardinals, finches, blue jays, and many other birds called from every branch, reminding me of my childhood love of birds. I hung a bird feeder in the yard and soon they arrived. Because nights were dark in Sea Cliff, I watched the star-filled sky and began to notice the moon's phases as it waxed and waned every month. I was surrounded by nature, wrapped in it. I asked for help. How do I nurture myself? Let me sit here until I learn.

When Jeremy had become sick, I felt the depth of pain and disease within my own mind. I started to reprogram the thoughts that assaulted me and prevented me from being alert to what I needed to understand.

I felt how healing it was to say the simple words, "I approve of myself." My cells relaxed as I spoke them over and over.

I loved Sea Cliff; I would always love it. My life transformed since moving there. The town emitted an energy that I had not felt anywhere else I'd lived. I was grateful for quiet misty mornings before the sun rose, for the damp smell of the earth after a rain, for the towering pines and the way the full moon shone through them onto the narrow, hilly streets lined with colorful bungalows, and for the stately Victorian homes on wide avenues.

Sea Cliff taught me about love and safety and trust. My intuition led me and I trusted it. Being around Puja for a few days each week and listening to her Scottish brogue opened me to new possibilities.

One morning while Puja made breakfast, she picked up a plate with rabbits painted around the edge that I used every morning. She put it down and said, "No, this is your special plate. I'll find another one." No one had ever been that tuned in, and I appreciated her for respecting my space. She was a non-intrusive presence in the cottage. I felt safe with our verbal agreement about living together with no signed lease. She offered me information and healing at my own pace, never forcing her knowledge on me.

Jeremy and I moved in July 1992 and that summer was a reprieve for us. Our future looked brighter. Jeremy's chemo and radiation were finished, but we still visited Sloan-Kettering for regular checkups and MRIs.

Sea Cliff—1992

HUDDLE

Jeremy's coordination deteriorated as the fall wore on. I knew something had happened one day when he arrived late to my design office in Port Washington after school. He had been in a car accident as he exited the highway. He didn't see the car on his right side—the side affected by the tumor. He wasn't injured, but his car was dented. I called the doctor and we went to Sloan for an MRI to explore what was happening. They sent us home to wait for the results.

Fall 1992 (journal entry)

It's almost a year since Jeremy got sick. I feel alone going through anniversary blues. I want comfort, need to be held and rocked. I feel stressed by my worries about Jeremy. In limbo. Is he getting better or worse? I want to feel positive but I'm struggling with a lot of feelings that I've held at bay for a long time. I feel burnt out, need some reassurance before I can go on. I wake each morning and feel I've been crying all night, my whole chest raw and on fire. Every muscle aches. I want to lean on someone. Jeremy and I huddle for safety. Who cares for the caretaker? I look around. People I know are having babies, leading normal lives, making plans for the future. We sit here dealing with this enormous outrage. I scream and cry with rage. Our life moves along, yet I'm powerless to control its direction. I am anguished, ripped off, and twitching with feelings. Sometimes I have to keep moving to discharge all this energy, other times I'm completely exhausted. Spent to the last drop.

My therapy group was one of the few places I felt safe to express my feelings. After Jeremy's first surgery, I shook with cold, huddled in the corner of the couch. Roger invited me to lie on the floor and asked everyone to kneel around me, putting their hands under my body to support me. Tears ran down my face and wet my hair. I looked up and saw their sadness.

After months and months of listening to everyone's normal neurotic concerns—a place I vaguely remembered—rage rose in me. Jeremy struggled and I was at my wit's end. When my turn came to speak, I looked around, furious at my life and what it had become. I spat out, "I hate you all. I hate you all for your normal lives. I hate you. Fuck you. Fuck your simple lives!"

Alice reached over and took my hand. Damon, in a whisper, said, "Let it out. Let it all out."

As a result of this last MRI, the doctors decided on a third exploratory surgery to clean out the accumulated dead matter after the radiation and chemotherapy. Jeremy was determined to take any opportunity available to heal. He agreed to the surgery.

I needed a break before Jeremy's next operation so I visited my friend Esther, my former counselor from Carrier Clinic, for a week. She'd moved to Florida earlier that year. When I flew back from Florida's warmth into La Guardia that December, I didn't even have a coat with me. *What was I thinking?*

The usual cordon of limo drivers thrust their placards in my face. Jeremy was supposed to pick me up. I scanned the faces in baggage claim. He wasn't there. *Did something happen?* I called home and listened to the phone ring.

He finally rushed through the automated door, flushed and out of breath, my black winter coat over his arm. He'd been on his own for the week I visited Esther. *Had it been stupid of me to leave him alone? Yet I'd also felt he needed time without me hovering over him.*

I thanked him for bringing my coat. He smiled and handed it to me.

When we arrived home, he insisted I come down to the basement. The basement of our rented cottage was dark, with shadows crawling forward from every corner. He flicked on a light I hadn't seen before.

My art table stood in the corner of the basement with paints and paper neatly arranged to one side. Without any place to work since we moved, I had stashed my paints in the closet and forgotten them.

"I thought you needed a place to do your art," was all he said. He'd rigged up a fluorescent light above the table and the corner looked inviting.

All his life he'd seen me painting or drawing. Jenny and he groaned when I tacked nude sketches in the corner of our Queens Village living room. What would their friends say? We had a running joke about Mr. Marblehead as they called a mannequin with marbles erupting from a hole in his head—one of the projects for my advanced graphic design course. At night they turned him to face the wall so they could walk through the living room without his eyes following them. These design courses, which I took at the School of Visual Arts after my first job, helped me grow in my profession and gave me the confidence to reach for more challenging work.

When I returned from Florida, I found out that Jake, my employer, was upset because I hadn't brought in enough business. For all of 1992 I was a full-time employee and worked hard to keep our big account despite the changes in Jeremy's condition. Jake decided to fire me the day I took Jeremy to Sloan for the intake before his next operation. Jeremy was scheduled for surgery shortly before Christmas. What was I going to do? No one hired around the holidays.

After our day in the hospital, we drove to my office. It was six o'clock. Shaking, I walked into Jake's office and shut the door. "You can't fire me now. I will not let you. After all the work I've done to win back our biggest account, where's your loyalty? You see what I'm going through!" My friends at work let him know that they supported me. I had nothing to lose, nowhere to go. Jake looked uneasy. He backed down and told me I could stay. The whole office followed Jeremy and me to a restaurant where I drank a glass of wine with my friends.

Despite our fears, we concentrated on positive talk while Jeremy prepared for surgery at North Shore Hospital. As he lay on the gurney outside the operating room, I kissed him and told him I would see him in a few hours. I drove home to find that Puja had cooked a dinner for her and me to share, a loving gesture that comforted me. We ate together at the dining room table. In her lilting Scottish brogue she told me how much Jeremy would love the apple turnovers I'd just removed from the oven. Their spicy cinnamon smell filled the house. I was grateful she was there; I didn't want to be alone. My body felt on fire, adrenaline pumped through my veins. Part of me paced the hospital corridor outside the operating room.

I returned to the hospital a few hours later. Vinny walked into the waiting room and found me already there. He could tell I was anxious from the way I picked at my fingers and rocked in my seat.

I felt so scared, I didn't want to deal with him. Although he wasn't much comfort, it was better than being alone. And he was Jeremy's father.

The doctor told us Jeremy was in recovery. They'd had to go deeper than they'd planned to clean out the tumor bed. Before he finished his sentence, I jumped up and asked to see Jeremy even though he was still groggy.

We followed him to the recovery room where Jeremy slept, his head bandaged. He moaned, "Ow, my head hurts," as if he was having a bad dream. I asked the nurse if he could have something for the pain and she gave him Tylenol.

Vinny's face was clenched, his lips a thin line. It was hard for him to see his son like this, but he said nothing. I began to cry, my anxiety rising. "Get a grip on yourself," he said.

Maureen gave Jenny and me our Christmas gifts early that year. It was late afternoon and the lights were already on at my house. Tomorrow I would bring Jeremy home from the hospital to recuperate.

Jenny stripped off her jeans and sweater in my bedroom, leaned over to put on her new pants. I stared at her body in the low light. I had no idea she was so thin, thinner than I'd ever seen her. Her shoulder blades stood out. The truth was hidden beneath her clothes. *Was she on a hunger strike in sympathy for her brother?* I asked her if she was eating, and she told me she didn't have much of an appetite. She drank a lot of coffee, ate when she could, which wasn't often.

Being so focused on Jeremy's care, I hadn't paid attention to Jenny. When she visited for the weekend, we didn't talk about what was going to happen to Jeremy. No one wanted to touch that one. Better to keep moving.

THE DOCTORS ALLOWED ME TO TAKE JEREMY HOME ONLY A FEW DAYS after surgery. His head was still bandaged. I made his bed on the living room couch and started a roaring fire in the fireplace. I cooked his favorite meal of veal cutlets, corn, and mashed potatoes, which he wolfed down. He had been through so much. What could I do to heal him? I saw the power of my love, the food, and our warm home. He sank into the love and respite I could provide, which would nurture him in ways that the hospital with all its medicine, operations, and efficient procedures couldn't.

This operation was supposed to clean out the tumor bed—such an ominous image, like washing a floor or brushing dead matter from the radiation away. The doctors were always positive, but underneath no one talked about the dread—the phone that took too long to ring with word from the lab. I busied myself cleaning the house and changing Jeremy's sheets. I shopped and cooked. My head pounded. My heart beat irregularly, my breath came fast even though I was not exerting myself. We kept busy—me with doing, he with TV and sleep, healing from this new assault on his brain.

By Monday I was furious with the doctors, imagined them busy with their lives while we hung suspended, holding our breaths. I called the hospital and asked to speak with the doctor. *What have you heard?*

I tried not to scream at him, but I wanted to reach through the phone and will the answer to be, *Everything will be all right.* I wanted to wring those words out of him. I wanted to will us back to normal life. But he said, "We haven't gotten the results back." I didn't know how to sit with the uncertainty one minute longer. And yet I must, we must.

I told Jeremy and we knew there'd be more waiting. The birds sang from far away in the trees as if all life was outside and we couldn't get there, not yet, maybe not anymore. And I hated how helpless I felt. I hated that I couldn't tell him it would be all right, because we were both grown-ups. So we watched *In Living Color,* sat close and hunkered down together in the pale winter light. What supported us now was the love we had for each other.

THE DOCTORS TOLD JEREMY THAT HE WOULD BE BACK TO NORMAL IN A week. They made it sound like such a breeze. The surgery went deeper than they expected, so it affected the motor functions on his right side.

By now, we had lived in Sea Cliff for six months. I felt the peaceful arms of this town holding us in her safe embrace.

Despite our uncertainty, we had a simple, wonderful Christmas that year. Every year since his appendectomy, Jeremy came with me to find the right tree. Christmas was his favorite holiday. Whatever tree I held up he rejected. "It's not big enough." "It's scrawny." That year, however, I shopped alone. I brought back the tree and decorated it myself while he lay on the couch.

On Christmas we exchanged fun gifts, simple gifts, gifts bought and given in love. I stood in line with Jeremy at Tower Records while he waited to buy a handful of CDs. When we opened our gifts, he and Jenny had bought me *Harvest Moon* by Neil Young. He kidded me, "You were standing with me in line when I bought it and you didn't even see it." They also gave me four blue Chinese bowls that Jenny had picked out in Chinatown.

Jeremy and I shopped for clothes to wear on Christmas Day. I held up a shirt, "How about this?"

He already had an armload of shirts. "It's purple."

"Just try it on with the other ones." When he came out of the dressing room wearing it, I said, "Wow! You look great."

He checked himself out in the mirror. He looked sophisticated, ready for a date. He tucked it into his pants.

"What do you think?" I asked.

"I like it."

It was the best Christmas I ever had—and the last we shared together as a family. The memories are a blessing. Holding onto them through the years made the shifts and changes easier.

That Christmas we shared laughter and familiarity, the familiarity of those who had lived together for many years and felt safe, loved, and able to be themselves.

Littleworth Lane, Sea Cliff—1993

HUNGER

Jenny and Jeremy left on Christmas for a few days with their father. I had my usual day-after-Christmas relaxation that consisted of lying in bed with a good book and eating leftovers. I walked the streets at dusk, a lone figure in the crisp cold. Stars dotted the dark sky, the rising moon shone from between tree branches. Houses were lit up and I smelled wood smoke. I was invited to a party that night given by Helene, a new acquaintance I'd met at my house when she came to see Puja.

At the party, I met Tony, the man who would figure prominently in my life for five years. I wasn't consciously looking. In fact I was content alone. I went to the party with no expectations, wondering what these people would be like.

Tony sauntered across the room trailing a woman still in conversation. He reminded me of a horse racing to the barn for food after a long ride—nothing could stop him. Raw hunger filled his eyes, as he looked me up and down. The woman sensed the conversation was over. Like snow on a July day, she melted away.

"Hi," he said in a deep voice. Dark hair framed his face. His eye-teeth, when he smiled, protruded as if he was ready to dip his face down to my neck and drink his fill.

And I, with a purple scarf wrapped around my neck, felt a strong desire to remove it like a last piece of clothing and reveal my white and waiting pulse.

The party swirled around us. We could have been standing in the middle of Times Square for all it mattered.

Most of his conversation teased with information that left out important details. He had five children. *Was he married?* His ex-wife was taking him to court. *Was he abusive? Did he intend to frighten me off?* But those eyes, that deep voice!

All evening he stayed with me, asking questions, clearly interested. Although I didn't want to admit it, I was too. I tasted adventure and something I was starved for—the promise of mystery, of flying free if only for a little while.

He walked me to my car and asked for my phone number. I handed him my business card.

RESPITE

Our first date was on a cold January night. We had dinner and saw *A Few Good Men*, then drove back to my house.

We kissed goodnight in his car and kept kissing, our warm lips meeting and his mustache scratching my upper lip. I nestled into his arms. I forgot how good it felt to be held. Our breaths created a mist that hid us from the outside world. Soft light from the streetlight glowed through the fogged-up windows. I opened up to a part of myself that had gone dead. I was on fire with the unexpected pleasure of his touch.

Loud rapping pulled us back. I turned to see a shadow on the car window. Then a voice, "Mom? Are you okay?"

I smoothed my hair and rolled down the window. Cold air rushed in like a slap. Jeremy's anxious face. "I was worried. Didn't know where you were. It's four o'clock."

My reassuring breathless words, "I'll be in soon. Go back inside; it's cold."

"I've got to go," I said to Tony.

"I want to make love to you," he whispered, the words themselves a caress.

Words I replayed over and over in my head all week.

Tony gave me directions to his house, fifty miles away. He stood in the doorway while I got out of my car. I walked around his house with my coat still on, drawn to the living room with the liquid sound of the tanks and stopped to stare at the moving fish.

He poured us both a glass of red wine, and we sat on the couch drinking. I took my coat off, "Your fish are beautiful." He didn't answer, put down his glass and kissed me. I kissed him back, then pushed him away. He held me and kissed my neck. I felt my body soften; maybe I could relax and abandon my life for a while. He stood up, held my hands and pulled me into the hallway.

What would he think if I gave in so easily? What would I think of myself? If I entered his bedroom, there was no turning back. It had been a year since I'd broken with Paul and years since I'd slept with another man. *Did I have the energy for this with Jeremy sick?* I hesitated on the threshold. I really couldn't back down now. I wanted him, and wanted to be held, but I didn't know him.

He wrapped me in his arms and I leaned into him, feeling my resistance leave. *Was it the wine?* He slowly walked backwards, pulling me into his bedroom. It was painted dark red, like the inside of a heart. He left to light the candle on his dresser. When he came back, he took me in his arms.

I circled my arms around his neck. *Yes, take me away; take me away.*

He kissed me. It felt like joy.

All day, we dressed and left the bedroom, only to return again, until finally he lit the wood stove in the living room. We lay naked in front of its warmth. Our bodies glowed orange from the flames, while the last rays of the sun flickered out and night descended. I grabbed a blanket from the couch and wrapped it around me.

"My God," I said, "we're lying in the ashes."

He laughed.

"I need to go home." I said.

"Stay."

"I have to get home to my son."

"He can take care of himself for the night."

"No he can't," I said, brushing ashes off my legs.

"Why?"
"It's a long story. Do you really want to hear?"
"Yes," he said, and sat up.

WILD

Some of my friends thought Tony was a loser: twice divorced with no profession. Even I, when I first met him, wondered *Why him?* I started seeing him anyway. I was beyond trying to figure anything out so I went with my heart. This was a wild time in my life and I was wild with emotion. Tony was untamed in his own way. He had the smell of smoke and the woods around him. He exuded a quiet wildness, a stubborn refusal to do anyone's bidding. We walked into the woods as if we were trying to escape the world and our lives.

He introduced me to Native American spirituality and the sweat lodge, to five-degree cold on a full-moon night in January. We strolled by the sea on sunset nights, watched the moon rise white over the blue water as the fiery sun set behind us. We burned fires, as if we needed more heat and more passion.

I was wild with grief, wild with a will to live that surprised me. I was no longer tame.

He came to hold my heart in his and maybe he felt at home with me, even though he didn't talk much. His eyes were dark and sparkling; he laughed although I knew the pain in his life. He was my lover, beyond what I believed I should have; perfect for that time in my life when everything turned upside down. Only I knew what I needed. My body knew. He set me on fire and I needed to burn, needed his arms to hold me. We were both on fire and if there is any truth to two souls finding each other at the right time, this was the proof.

Sea Cliff—1993

UGLY

The green rubber Gumby twisted into the "fuck you" gesture, so ubiquitous in New York, gave voice to Jeremy's bravery—and his humor. It was safer to hide behind laughter. His teachers at open-school night always commented on his humor—the class clown—but he didn't apply himself. I'd fed him that bravery with his baby food. Now bravery gave way to reality and we watched comedy videos. We lay on his bed every night laughing, which was safer than crying. We didn't show our tears or our fears to each other. With us, courage moved us forward—a united phalanx. *How else to face it?*

Yet after we moved to Sea Cliff, Jeremy approached me, saying, "I need a hug." I was always available for this tenderness.

I made a choice and now wonder when I did. *When was the moment I accepted that I had no control over what was happening to my son?*

For years I worked to keep my life in balance, not taking on too much because I didn't trust that I could handle it after my breakdown. I kept my defenses up. Yet my love for Jeremy drew me beyond all my limits and transformed me. This was my choice.

When 1993 began, we realized that Jeremy's recuperation from the December operation would not be swift, despite the doctor's reassurances. He walked with an awkward gait, landing hard on his left foot as if he couldn't judge where the floor was. It took him forever to tie his shoes.

I heard him in his room, screaming at the football game on TV. "Oh, what's the matter? Throw the damn ball already! You stupid fucking losers!" I heard him stomp across his floor; then something hit the wall. "Goddamn it!" I heard the helpless fury in his voice.

The doctors said the tumor bed was clean, yet he still wasn't right. They kept performing MRIs. *Is it growing or is it just dead tissue?* His life constricted and he stayed home, unable to drive. I took him with me whenever I could. He waited in an eddy while life flowed on.

We arrived at Sloan for a big conference to review the latest MRIs. He always passed his neurological tests, showing his physical strength to the doctors to prove he was okay. The doctor put up the latest MRI. He talked with Vinny and me about the changes and what they meant. The operation went deep into his brain. I saw the changes going even deeper, penetrating further into his life force. It looked ugly.

Jeremy, on the examining table, peeked around the edge of the curtain for the first time to see what we talked about. He seemed hesitant, like someone peering into that dark closet to see what lurked there. Looking at his future as if a crystal ball floated inside his head.

On the way home from work a few weeks later, I watched the houses slip by the train window. The balance of Jeremy's life seemed tentative. I used my will to hold my fear at bay. So much energy went into trusting that our world wouldn't fall apart. Between my eyes, the tension throbbed. My fear led me to imagine Jeremy at home doing his homework.

STUTTER

Jeremy's brain fires ideas at him; he writes on the white paper in front of him. Then he stops mid-word as it all falls apart—the attic room, his hands as he notices them shaking. His body convulses as he slides from the wooden chair, moving in a dance he doesn't understand. His head jerks forward and back, his body vibrates like a jackhammer. His words Oh, shit, shit, shit lost as each letter rocks like a Cubist painting, devolving as it leaves his stuttering mouth. His body is a puppet controlled by his brain gone wild. He feels the nap of the rug against his face—if he can only hold on. Then he doesn't wonder anymore. He recedes from his body into a world with no meaning and worse—he is alone. At any moment without warning, his brain, already wounded, can come completely undone.

The sunlight moves across his room, low now in the sky, shining into his eyes. He sweats, lying on his side under the desk. At first he can't move his arms. How did he get here? He feels warm drool sliding out of his mouth. He reaches his hand up and takes a swipe, nearly misses his mouth. He stares at his hand. Red. His tongue tastes metal. Slowly his brain rearranges itself; thoughts come back.

No sound but the steady tick of the clock, a car accelerates in the distance.

THE FOLLOWING WEEK, JUST AS I FEARED, JEREMY HAD A SEIZURE WHILE home alone. He was shaken and I was too. I couldn't be home all the time since I worked; still, I felt awful. I didn't want him to face this alone. About a week later, as I talked with him on the living room couch, he began to have a seizure. Horrified, I watched as he stuttered and his face and body twitched uncontrollably. I held his head and wondered what to do. *Should I grab his tongue? Would he swallow it?* I wanted to scream for help but stayed there. As quickly as the seizure started, it ended, and he returned to normal. Again we were both shaken. The physical manifestations of the cancer were hard to ignore.

A few days later, on Sunday, he began running a fever. I called Sloan-Kettering and spoke to Mary, the assistant assigned to us. Normally, they rushed patients right in. Since I was very knowledgeable about all his medications and knew how to handle a crisis, she said to monitor him and keep in phone contact. By early evening his fever had risen. Mary said to rush him in. I settled Jeremy in the passenger's seat, reclined it back, and told him to hang on.

The Long Island Expressway was bumper to bumper as it frequently was. I drove the right shoulder past traffic. I made good time until I came to a parked police car. He flagged me down and shone a flashlight in. I said "It's an emergency, I need to get my son to the hospital." He looked at Jeremy and saw I was telling the truth. "Why didn't you call an ambulance?" he asked. "Because I need to get to Sloan-Kettering in

Manhattan, not a local hospital." He waved us on. I sped into Manhattan. Another night at the hospital.

I called Jenny and also Vinny. Other than that, I handled this and many other challenges alone. Sometimes, people were at work or it was quicker to get in the car and go myself. But the truth was that I was used to handling things alone all these years. I had no concept of the support and comfort I might be missing. However, we were lucky that Vinny had good medical coverage. Between his and Kyle's policies, most of Jeremy's huge bills were paid.

AFTER THEY TOOK BLOOD AND CHECKED HIS VITAL SIGNS, THEY HOOKED up an IV drip with antibiotics. Jenny walked into the ER, dressed in sweat pants, sneakers, and a T-shirt, her hair pulled back in a ponytail. She'd walked the twenty blocks from her apartment. It was after ten. She sat down on his bed. "Hey, Jer, how you doing?"

He shrugged and gave her a weak smile.

"Thanks for coming," I said. I handed her a Coke. She rubbed her eyes.

"What were you doing?" he asked.

"I was watching TV when Mom called. How do you feel?" she asked.

"Like shit."

She looked over at me. "They have to keep him here until his fever goes down," I said.

She put her hand on his forehead. "He doesn't feel so warm."

"I'm tired," he said.

"Why don't you close your eyes and try to sleep," she said.

A little later, while he still slept, she and I walked into the hallway. "Why don't you go home; it's late. You have work tomorrow."

"I'll stay for awhile," she said.

It felt good to have her there.

After Jenny left I dozed, back in the twilight world of the early morning hospital. I heard the hum of machines and occasional loudspeaker messages calling for doctors. I couldn't find a place of comfort on the bedside chair. Early in the morning the nurse took Jeremy's temperature and the doctor on call checked him. His temperature was normal so they released him. We drove back to Sea Cliff going against the flow of morning commuters headed to Manhattan.

We hadn't eaten since yesterday so we stopped at the deli on Main Street for donuts and sandwiches. A few patrons emerged with their morning coffee. Kids walked towards school with backpacks slung across their shoulders—normal life.

ALL THROUGH EARLY 1993 WE SHUTTLED BACK AND FORTH BETWEEN Sea Cliff and Sloan-Kettering for MRIs, blood tests, and checkups. Some weeks we drove in more than once. I scheduled checkups towards the end of the day so we could meet Jenny at her apartment. They couldn't decide if Jeremy was improving. Even with frequent MRIs nothing was clear.

But slowly he recovered, weaned himself off the steroids that gave him a round moon face. He began to drive again, returned to school, and visited his friend Sean. I had more free time to spend with Tony. By March he felt the best he had in a long time. We were more hopeful than we'd been in the past few months; maybe he was finally on the mend.

> *I stood in the bathroom doorway and watched Jeremy examine himself in the mirror, as he used to do when he fixed his hair, smoothing it down so not a strand was out of place. I found it hard to see the changes, the hair on the right side that wasn't going to grow back—all that radiation or the pellets they drilled into his skull killed it. His scar traced a drunken backwards C. It circled the whole right side of his head. If he turned sideways and looked from the left side, he looked as he always had except when his hair fell out during chemo. Now he turned that way and studied his image—thinner than before, definitely more serious, not innocent*

anymore. He turned to the right side. No, everything had changed. That's why he wore the baseball cap everywhere.

To me he looked beautiful.

He was here.

Sea Cliff—1993

GIFT

Tony seemed content to embrace me as either friend or lover. After his two stormy marriages, our relationship must have felt like an oasis. Although we fought, or at least I fought with him when he pissed me off, I always returned. In the past, once I left, a relationship was over. I even prided myself on my ability to shut the door and keep it closed. Not with Tony. I came back because his arms comforted me, though there were deeper needs he couldn't satisfy. Maybe my dream of emotional closeness was just that. He and I shared intense experiences that I'd never had with any previous partner. He walked with me through Jeremy's illness, held my hand, and balanced the dark. We had fun and sex was better than any time before. We barely entered my house before ripping each other's clothes off. Our desire went beyond words, primal, necessary, maybe the only way to balance the enormity of what was unfolding.

He was present for me. I think it took his mind off his own troubled divorce.

He arrived ten months before Jeremy died: a surprise, an unexpected gift. At first I couldn't pay attention. I was overwhelmed, short, and angry. He didn't run, whatever his flaws as I perceived them. He stayed until the end, telling me "I'm not going anywhere." I had never been supported like that before. I thought, *This is what it's supposed to feel like.*

I showed up with all my wounds and sometimes acted as if he was the only one who needed to change. After Paul, I was determined not to hold my feelings in.

Tony listened to me rage. He'd had enough fighting and anger in his life, he said. What was I like before Jeremy got sick? Was I less angry?

"Not by much," I replied.

See, There He Is

I WALKED WITH JEREMY THROUGH THE STREETS OF SEA CLIFF ALMOST every day in early 1993, so he could strengthen his body after his last surgery. The afternoon sun came through the trees, leaving dappled patterns on the sidewalk as we strolled to the Point. His foot thumped with every step, reminding us he wasn't back to normal. That day we talked about his dream of becoming a doctor, which meant transferring to Hunter College to take pre-med courses. We applied past the deadline, but a friend pushed his application through anyway. We agreed that he needed to live in the college dorms rather than travel every day. In case of an emergency, he would also be close to Sloan-Kettering

He didn't decide until he finished his first year of college what he wanted to major in. I understood his interest—he'd been in and out of hospitals for two years. He'd make an excellent doctor, certainly a very caring one.

Jenny watched him. One day she said to me, "If Jeremy can go to college even though he's sick, I've got no excuse for not finishing high school." She started studying for her high school diploma.

DESPERATE

I STILL WORKED FOR JAKE, TWENTY MINUTES AWAY IN PORT WASHINGTON. We had recently finished a project and I was home for two weeks, feeling uneasy. Although we had redesigned the corporate publication I worked on, the client hinted at another change. Then, in early spring, Jake called to tell me our client had cancelled the account. My fears were realized; I found myself out of work.

I bought a pack of cigarettes and sat on the porch steps, smoking one after another, drinking wine straight out of the bottle. Jeremy found me there. He picked up the cigarettes and asked what was the matter. I told him. He asked what I was going to do now. I shrugged my shoulders.

He sat down and put his arm around me. I was reminded of how he held me when my friend Jonathan had died—unasked, silent—putting his arms around me as I sobbed. No questions, no embarrassment, he just showed up with his big gentle heart.

The *New York Times* ran ads every week for graphic production work, always available, but requiring a one and one-half hour commute each way into Manhattan. I didn't like being so far from Jeremy yet I needed money. Right now. I called one company and they asked me to come in for an interview.

I parked at a meter and Jeremy waited in the car. I said it wouldn't take long, but the receptionist asked me to wait. The people next to me were applying for clerical or office cleaning jobs. I wanted to bolt. I was concerned that the police would tow my car, yet something told me to wait.

Finally I was called into a back office, rented by a woman who hired graphic artists. After interviewing me, she said she'd be in touch. I hoped I didn't look desperate. I raced downstairs; two hours had passed. A cop had attempted to give me a ticket, and Jeremy talked him out of it, saying his mother was upstairs at a job interview. In Manhattan that was a miracle.

The company called with weekend work at a Madison Avenue ad agency. I was nervous because I didn't have much computer experience. I spent Saturday faking it. I didn't want to ask the other designers questions because they'd see I was inexperienced. I retreated to the bathroom to study the computer instruction book I'd brought with me. I expected them to kick me out, but they asked me to return on Sunday.

Next I worked for a pharmaceutical ad agency, filling in for a woman out sick for a week. I worked in a roomful of other production designers. Again I was nervous about my skills.

However, at the end of the week Oscar, my boss, sat down in the chair next to me as I filled out my time sheet, and asked me to come back the following week. I tried to hide my surprise. He put his arms behind his head and regarded me from behind his glasses, saying he could use an additional designer. I said yes.

JEREMY FEARS

My mother worked from as far back as I can remember. We didn't live with Dad so she supported us. When I was a little boy, I used to run screaming after her when she left for work. Then she'd start to cry. I never told her how scared I was that she wouldn't come back.

Now lying in my room, I wonder when she'll be home. I start feeling scared like I always did when she left me alone, but I try to talk myself out of it. You know, I'm too big for this. I do what I always did. I pick up the phone, dial the number Mom left, and ask for her. The woman on the other end hesitates and my heart leaps. "Oh, the new designer. Just a minute." Silence. Then Mom's voice saying hello. I let my breath out. Can you bring some ice cream home? I have to come up with a reason for the call even though she doesn't mind. Now I ask her the question I really want to know. When is she coming home? She says she is leaving in an hour, which means it will be close to three hours before she gets here. Then we say goodbye with the little game we play. She says, "You hang up first." But I can't. I wait.

"Jer, you still there?"
"Yeah."
"You go first."
"Okay. Bye for now." I put the phone down.

TREADMILL

We were at the hospital again; it seemed like every week—examinations, blood tests, and neurological reviews.

The news was never good. We drove in with hope in the backseat, came home with reality in charge. *Leave us alone to enjoy our life here behind the trees, far away from the doctors!* I gripped the wheel; we were stuck in traffic again. Jeremy ate the sandwich I bought him before we merged onto the FDR Drive. I was too tired and anxious to eat.

What kind of treadmill from hell were we on? I wanted to sit on the porch listening to the wind and the birds. I wanted to be held in nature's quiet embrace. I really couldn't go on. Jeremy looked wiped. We moved forward because we must.

Back home, I could hear music from his room, De La Sol on loud. I sat on the porch, rocking, rocking, my mind blank. *How would I ever get up and fix dinner? Would someone please come and tell me this is a dream I will wake up from?*

Sea Cliff—1993

GROWING

In May they called us back to Sloan-Kettering for another MRI. A few days later, I phoned Dr. Walker for the results. This time the news was bad. Although the tumor bed was clean after the last operation, the cancer now grew in another direction. Our world collapsed. I asked Dr. Walker what we should do. She said if Jeremy were her son, she would take him home and enjoy him for as long as possible. I felt our lives spin out of control.

Again I was the messenger with bad news. I called Vinny and we had another family conference at Sloan. Jeremy wanted to continue fighting. Another doctor was brought in who wanted to use aggressive chemotherapy to see if it could shrink the tumor. If it did, they would attempt a bone marrow transplant. They sent us home with instructions to build Jeremy up and take some time to rest. They planned to start treatments in August.

When I'd found out the tumor was growing, I'd paged Tony. He'd just arrived at his mother's house where he was spending the night. He said, "I'm on my way." Jeremy was in the kitchen when I heard Tony's car pull up. I went to stand on the porch. He rushed up the walk, opened his arms, and said, "Oh baby, what a cross you have to bear." I slipped inside the circle of his arms and leaned against his chest sobbing, his strong body held me up. I looked over Tony's shoulder and saw Jeremy inside the screen door, watching.

Now I wonder if what he saw told him the whole story. He was leaving and his mother knew it. The doctors would do what they could. He was alone on the other side of the screen.

By now I worked full time with Oscar. When Jeremy or the hospital needed to reach me, they called on the only phone in the production room. I tried to be discreet and not say much or stay on the phone too long, but it was hard to conceal that a crisis was going on. My experience was that busy New York businesses didn't want to hear about their employees' personal problems.

After a few days of this, Oscar asked to see me and motioned to an empty office. I entered and he closed the door. *This is it,* I thought. *He's going to fire me.*

He faced me, "I don't know what's going on in your life and I don't need to know. I just want you to know you always have work here. If you need to take time off, that's fine. I'll work with you."

It took a few minutes for me to realize he wasn't firing me. "Oscar, my son has brain cancer," I blurted. I wanted to reach out and hug him.

He seemed shocked by my words and touched my arm. "I'm sorry to hear that. Don't worry about work."

After that, he gave me assignments that didn't require me to work late like some of the other production people. Now that I had an advocate, it was easier to come to work every day. Once a week Jeremy came into the city because he was seeing my therapist, Roger. After his session he came to my office and waited for me in the reception room. He wanted to meet Oscar, but I felt awkward and never invited him to come upstairs. I didn't want to cause a fuss. Now I regret that decision. It would've been better if they had met.

On these days Jenny met us downstairs and we traveled to her apartment on East 81st Street. It almost seemed normal—a family meeting for dinner in New York. It was sweet to be together with my adult children, all of us present and alive, eating food and laughing. Jenny opened the French doors of her studio, and we watched people walk down the street as we sat on her bed. I have a photo of the three of us crowded into the picture frame laughing, Jeremy with two fingers up making horns behind Jenny's head.

Later, she told me her role was to give Jeremy hope, to share her world and show him the possibility of a future after the treatments ended. She breezed into our everyday reality with stories and jokes, entertained and kidded him like when they were younger. She didn't express her fears and worries, although he expressed his fears of dying to her—fears he and I didn't share with each other. I knew my role was to lend him strength, not burden him with my emotions. Now I wish we could've spoken how we truly felt, but I was afraid it would be too much and he, or maybe I, wouldn't be able to go on.

UGH

Puja had given me information about an herbal treatment called Essiac that helped some cancer patients kill their tumors. I sent away to Canada for a five-pound bag. The instructions on the bag said it must be boiled and strained through stainless steel instruments. I bought what I needed and mixed up a batch. I told Jeremy about the tea and he agreed to try it.

However, when he came into the kitchen, he wrinkled his nose. "What the hell is that awful smell?"

"It's the herbal tea I brewed for you."

"I'm not drinking that."

No persuasion on my part made him change his mind. We faced each other, arms crossed.

"You drink it first," he said.

"How about we drink it together."

He nodded with a half smile. I poured out two cups of the foul-smelling liquid and handed him a cup. I raised it to my lips and gulped it down. "Ugh!"

He drank his. "That's disgusting!"

We laughed.

At the end of May I attended my second Gestalt therapy weekend with Roger, two of his colleagues, and people from their various practices.

I remembered the transformation that resulted from the first weekend two years ago. I'd worked on my relationship with Paul, expressing how unhappy I was. However, the big breakthrough came when I'd worked with the other participants—doctors and businessmen and women—and realized from their emotional work how similar our deep wounds were. All the years since Carrier Clinic I'd felt the stigma of "being crazy," an outcast from normal society. During the weekend, many of my fellow therapy partners had asked me to be part of their healings. The therapists told me I was a very motivated special person. Because of this experience, I had begun to see my hospital stay as a breakthrough not a breakdown—my very sane desire to heal the past in order to go forward. I began to let go of my shame.

When Roger suggested that Jeremy join the second Gestalt weekend, I was reluctant because it was a place where I could release my feelings. I was concerned that with Jeremy present I wouldn't be able to do that. Also I needed a break from his care. At the same time, I wanted Jeremy to have this experience. Roger arranged for Jeremy to drive up and room with another young man to give me my own space. I agreed.

After we arrived, I didn't spend much time with Jeremy. The days were long, with each participant creating a center where they worked with their therapist, inviting chosen group members to play supportive roles. These centers enabled us to explore our emotional issues and get the support we needed to shift past wounds. They were emotionally intense and I watched Jeremy absorb the drama. He declined to have a center. Friday and Saturday passed without my taking a turn.

I felt anxious. How would this happen? I didn't want Jeremy to be present because I wasn't sure what would come out. I didn't want him to know how scared I was. Once I expressed this to Roger, he asked that Jeremy leave when my turn came.

On Sunday afternoon I found the courage to step up. Roger motioned Jeremy's roommate to sit opposite me on the floor and whispered instructions to him. He held my hands and said, "Mom, you need to let me go. You've helped me and I'm grateful, but you need to release me to live my own life."

I was shocked at his words and began to sob. "I'm afraid if I let you go, you'll die!" I had spoken my greatest fear out loud, as if I could keep death at bay by silence.

Again he said, "Mom, you need to let me go."

I could hear people in the room crying.

"You're so sick! Will you be all right if I let you go?"

I was relieved to express my deep fears. At least now they were in the open. I felt very close to Jeremy. Even though he didn't take a center, I knew he learned from watching others in such raw emotional states. As we drove back to Sea Cliff, we sang along to the radio and laughed. We were lighter—for now.

Sea Cliff—1993

FOG

Jeremy opens the front door and steps onto the porch. A cool morning breeze ruffles his hair. Summer is not his favorite season; misty fog and bracing cold suit him better. His attic room is hot and stuffy from yesterday's heat. Out here he feels alive. He can almost forget his head, the sharp pains, and seizures.

He shoves his feet into his sneakers and shuffles down the driveway past his car. The mist rises from the blacktop and he steps into it. The fog moistens his face and hair, glows with the hidden sun. He walks toward the light, kicking the leaves. He thinks of the foggy nights on Cape Cod, the quiet broken by water lapping the shore.

He traces a path down Littleworth Lane and turns right onto the road that leads to the golf course. When he takes a step, his left leg hits the ground before he expects, as if he used to be taller and now has shrunk.

He reaches the fence that surrounds the golf course and slips through the hole on his hands and knees, the wet grass cool on his palms. Mist rises off the greens. Ghostly trees appear and disappear. He hears crows up ahead, loud. A few call back from behind him. He feels the grass change under his feet, become smooth. He knows he is on the green. He lies down and spreads his arms out. The cool dew soaks through his clothes.

He feels his heart beating and wonders how much longer it will. What will it feel like to have all this fade away? No, he doesn't want to think about it.

What's the point? He feels like he's off on the sidelines of life anyway, just taking up space, being a burden. Oh, his mother denies it when he says that, but he feels like a burden to himself, unable to find a way out of the fog his life has become. He wishes he could rise up like the crows and fly free, leave his body lying on the green, near the hole. He can't even remember what he used to feel like before he got sick, when his body carried him without thought.

SWELTER

The summer of 1993 was hot. I walked around in shorts and a T-shirt, sweating. Even though Dr. Walker had advised us otherwise, Jeremy rested and gathered strength, preparing for more chemo. The summer provided a respite.

I worked for Oscar during the week, commuting to Fifth Avenue and 15th Street in Manhattan every day. I walked out of the cool lobby into blinding sun, heat, noise, and a stream of people flowing up and down the Manhattan streets. The heat surrounded my body. Sweat poured down my face. I made money for my son and me, commuted by subway to Pennsylvania Station and the Long Island Railroad's Port Washington line, exited at Little Neck, walked to my car, and drove twenty-five minutes to Sea Cliff. When I saw the water, my body relaxed. I was almost home, just around the harbor, past the beach, up the hill, and all the way to the end of Littleworth Lane. Trees blew in the hot wind but number forty was shaded. Jeremy's black Dodge Charger sat in the driveway.

On this day, he reclined on the lounge chair drinking soda. The porch was cooler than his attic room. Bonnie trotted down the stairs to greet me. I petted her. I scanned Jeremy; today he looked good. My eyes detected small changes. I looked for tired lines, but there were none that day.

All I wanted was to hang out with him. Dinner was simple; I had no energy for anything elaborate. Our oasis was hot, humid, and safe. I longed to take my work clothes off, but first I asked him about his day. He'd hung out all day because it was too hot to go to Sean's.

I changed into shorts and sat on the porch with cold lemonade, looking out at the street behind the screen of trees. A hot wind blew around the corner of the porch. I was too exhausted to move. We sat together not saying much, mesmerized by the rhythm of the rocking chair. There were phone calls to make and dinner to prepare, but not yet—the routine of a quiet cherished summer—hot, miserable, and precious—our last together.

On Friday night Tony arrived for the weekend. Saturday was even hotter, close to one hundred. Mid afternoon I stood on the porch and announced to no one in particular that I hoped we had a violent thunderstorm to break the heat. Later the breeze picked up, the sky grew dark, and thunder rumbled in the distance. Something big was coming. Now there was more wind, blowing hard, and more crashes of thunder. The first fat drops splattered on the hot sidewalk and vaporized. The three of us watched from the porch. At some point I heard the radio stop and knew the power had gone out.

The rain poured down in a fury. The storm blew through, leaving downed trees in its wake. Rivers gurgled through the streets. Quiet returned, but water sounds were everywhere. Steam rose from once-hot tar. No relief—it was more humid and no electricity to boot. Jeremy called Sean. They had power in Freeport. He climbed into his car and I waved as he drove off.

August came and my friend asked me to design a prototype catalog for her client. A week later she told me we were hired. I started the work, but soon realized it was more than I could handle in the evening. I told Oscar I had another project and needed to leave.

In early August Jeremy entered Sloan for the first round of the new chemo. He was very sick, hunched over the hospital bed vomiting. I worked at home during the day and commuted into Manhattan to stay with him at night. Every morning I drove home after getting him settled and went back to work. In the evening I walked into his hospital room. He was alone. Chemical odors rose off his body as I leaned to kiss his pale face. He was losing his hair again.

He was too sick to do much, just stared at the TV flashing *Wheel of Fortune* from the corner. My ears filled with hospital sounds, cars honking from the street seven floors below. There was not much nurture or comfort here. He left after a week, and came home to recuperate. I cooked his favorite foods to build him up. When his platelets reached forty, he would return for another round. I looked at him, knowing the chemicals would kill him before they killed the cancer.

He didn't have much energy. He lay around, waiting. I worked, driving the ninety minutes into Manhattan for meetings. Jenny was coming for the weekend. I brought food, goodies, and their favorite treat—ice cream.

Bless the ice cream, the sacrament of our time together. Bless St. Ben and St. Jerry and Jerry with his cherry. Bless the nights on the couch hanging out with my children in Sea Cliff, each with our own pint softening before us. Jeremy's was chocolate chip, each chip slowly dislodged from the frozen cream, popped into his mouth. Jenny preferred Mint Oreo, holding the frosty container as the ice melted and pooled in her lap; or me with New York Super Fudge Chunk, savoring every bite, holding it in my mouth until it ran cool down my throat. No one talked as we dipped spoonfuls of joy and licked the spoons, eating until we could hear the scrape of metal against empty. Blessed cows, with their rich cream and, oh, yes, chocolate, which takes away all pain, and nuts crunching between my teeth, releasing their flavor.

Jenny sighed, put down the spoon. "Remember when you brought ice cream home and the tops of the containers were already melting? Remember how you ate the soft top layer on each container before you put it into the freezer?"

"After hours of shopping, it was my reward."

We had an unspoken rule in our house. Whoever didn't finish their pint in two days was just about saying, "It's up for grabs." Most of the time it didn't last the first day.

JENNY BROUGHT HER WASH AND NEEDED A RIDE TO THE LAUNDROMAT. Now that we lived in a large house with a porch, she frequently came to spend the weekend; the three of us together again just like old times. We wandered the aisles at Tower Records, scanning the rock section. Jeremy carried an armload of CDs, laughing over the name of the group, Butthole Surfers. Young guy humor. I had fun looking for the most outrageous covers. The cashier had black spiked hair; he was pale, very Goth, with tattoos. We looked bland in comparison, but I wasn't focused on him. I searched for Jenny, who had been in the rap section, but now she wasn't in the store. I spied her through the window, smoking. I knew it pissed Jeremy off.

She wanted to go to the mall. I wanted to sit down and rest. Jeremy was along for the ride. Long Island on a Saturday—I couldn't stand it. Trapped in suburban numbness, I couldn't wait to return to my Sea Cliff oasis. I asked Jeremy if he had decided what to buy. It was our turn to check out. The sun hung low in the sky and I tried to remember where I parked the car. No matter what we bought, it wouldn't make us feel any better.

We left Tower. Jenny leaned against the store. "C'mon let's go. We've each got a video for tonight."

Back home she and he talked and listened to the CDs in his room. No longer in high spirits, we just slogged through the heat waiting for something to break. Tony was coming over. I wasn't sure if Jenny liked him, but he comforted me. She viewed him as an outsider, not really part of our family. She grudgingly accepted him because I was in a relationship with him. She mocked him, as if asking, *Are you good enough for my mother?* He gave as good as he got.

One day after our long ride into the city for blood tests, Jeremy and I collapsed on the couch, sweating. He tilted his head against the back of the couch, looking at the ceiling. The house was silent except for the murmur of our parakeets, Perry and Cecil. "I guess I won't be going to Hunter this fall." True, but not what I wished to contemplate.

By the end of August Jeremy felt better, but still looked pale. How much more could his body take? He was scheduled to return to Sloan after Labor Day for the second round of chemo.

I was near the end of my catalog project and it had been grueling—long hours and not much sleep. I decided to visit Robbie for the weekend to rest before the next onslaught. Jenny agreed to stay with Jeremy while I was gone.

On my birthday, Jenny and Jeremy brought me a piece of cake and sang *Happy Birthday*. I opened my gift from them, two tickets to a Sade concert. Jeremy's credit card was in the birthday card with a funny note to please return after I paid for the tickets. I could see by his smile how grown up he felt lending me his credit card. We ate cake, talked, and then I had to finish my work. It was the last birthday I spent with Jeremy.

When Jenny's boyfriend came over, I was still at work. I waved hello, my hair in disarray. I hadn't showered and wore the wrinkled clothes I had slept in. I cursed into the phone at the messenger service because they were late. I wondered what kind of first impression I made.

I said goodbye to my children. Three days of rest awaited me at Robbie's house. *I couldn't be responsible for another minute!* On the highway I put my foot to the floor and arrived at her house in record time.

When Jeremy became sick I wondered if Robbie would stand by me. Our friendship had never been tested before. We'd been friends for seven years; now to my grateful surprise, she became the friend I called the most. She checked on me regularly. We had always been able to share our deepest feelings. Time spent with Robbie was healing, her home felt like an oasis where I could relax into the familiar rhythm of our friendship. We met while working for the same design firm. We kept in touch after she, and then I, moved to new jobs. When her mother was diagnosed with breast cancer, I listened to her fears. Most visits turned into weekend-long talk marathons involving good food and wine; we smoked into the night in front of her fireplace. That day I couldn't wait to fall into her caring arms.

I paced Robbie's kitchen, gulping a glass of wine as I told her how insane my last two weeks had been. I lit one of her cigarettes and drank another glass of wine. She fixed me a plate of food, took my arm and led me to the table. I ate so fast I hardly tasted it. She listened until I was done.

She suggested we go into the living room where I leaned back on her couch and passed out.

When I returned home, Jenny pulled me aside. "Ma, I didn't realize how sick Jeremy was until I stayed with him. I'm afraid he's going to die."

I wasn't ready to accept that yet.

SUCKING

I don't even have to make myself disappear. It's happening as I watch. I see my ribs, my hipbones. I no longer drive, so I wait.

The trees are moving towards fall, turning red. I sit on the porch, the day quiet after the kids have gone to school. Peaceful. Puja works so I'm not alone, but soon she'll leave. I think about Cape Cod, the ocean, and the gulls. Think about Sean away at college, busy. I could walk around town but I'm too weary for that. I feel like it's all come to a halt. Too tired to figure it out. I'm waiting for new chemo that might do the trick. Everyone tries to help. I'm doing whatever they say. Following the rules although they keep changing.

I don't want to be here.

Mom will be home in a few hours. She's always busy, bustling around like she's going somewhere. She'll keep me safe. She knows how to fight. Mostly I feel like a burden, can't do much. Can't work. My life sucks right now. Just waiting. Don't know what for. It's warm on the porch, with just enough breeze. I wanted to live in a house more like my Dad's more modern one, but this musty old house is okay. Don't want to think about anything. When I do, it feels scary, like the dark.

RECEDE

The day before Jeremy returned to the hospital, we gathered at a French restaurant to celebrate Sean's father's fiftieth birthday. Jenny, Jeremy, Tony and I drove over. We knew most of the family and friends. Many asked Jeremy how he was doing. He smiled, full of bravado, talked about the food and joked with his friends. He was part of life, although I realized the vast gap between his everyday reality that he was gamely bridging and the world of people not facing their deaths. Food was a safe topic. He just wanted to be one of the guys—not different in this way.

I could only imagine what the world looked like to him. Everyone was tan and pink-cheeked, with plans for the next day that didn't include needles filled with chemicals. Plans for the future or next year easily slipped from young mouths unable to imagine what it felt like to be drifting away on an outgoing tide, watching familiar shores recede.

We played the game of keeping our faces presentable to the world, to not cause people to reel back at the intensity of our emotion. We rode a boat crafted to keep us on top of the vast deep ocean of feelings. The water was smooth on top, and we rode in faith into the unknown, refusing to look at the approaching wall of water. We sat together in the boat, focused on what was immediately around us—dinner with friends, a celebration—living right here.

We said goodbye. For many, it was the last time they saw Jeremy. They hugged him and sent him home surrounded by their love and warm wishes. My pale bald child had grown into manhood these last two years as his body failed him, failed to support his journey into the future. The cells of his brain forgot to stop growing and die. They had no boundaries.

Jenny's Story, Manhattan—1993

SMOKE

Jenny's mind was quick, her wit too. She talked circles around other people who were slower to understand. She moved fast, but came up against her brother's illness and was speechless. Rap songs, her *X-Files*, her Anne Rice vampire books, none of them gave her solace. She moved even quicker, moving faster than her emotions, which hadn't caught up with her. I realized I had taught her well.

Every day she left the sanctuary of her ground-floor studio apartment on the Upper East Side and walked into the pulsing life of Manhattan. She looked like any other pretty woman heading off to work, except she had a secret. Her life used to be about her boyfriend or where she and her friends were meeting on Friday night. This night she would go to the hospital to see her brother. He was twenty blocks south of her, not free to come and go.

What did she think as she caught the subway? How did she cope with the enormity of her dread? She could no longer pretend he would be okay, and the treats she gave herself in the past to carry her through hard times couldn't even begin to touch the empty hole inside her. At times I have been her, have watched life move uncontrollably towards an outcome I have pushed away, knowing I must surrender but not sure how.

> *I imagined her, as the stations flash by the subway windows, the people a blur, bracing her feet as she hurls forward.*
>
> *She remembers a time when she believed her brother would get better. Of course he would. He would leave home like she has. Maybe go to college. On summer break, he'd drive down to her apartment, and they'd have a few drinks at the corner hangout. They'd talk about music and what classes he was taking. Her boyfriend would meet them and they'd go for pizza. Life would go on. Today and yesterday would fade into a memory that they'd refer to*

as "that time" or "before you got better."

She shakes her head as if to shake free the thoughts because they aren't real. They are the dream she creates to push away for a few moments the hard truth that her brother isn't coming into the future with her. Forever, there will be a hole where he should have stood next to her. Her memories are what she will have left.

The sidewalk pitches and rolls, unsteady under her feet. Jenny stares bewildered at the insistent life of the city, its clear movement; everyone looks like they have purpose and a destination. No one strolls. She falters for a moment, forgetting what street she is on until she sees the coffee shop at the end of the block and realizes she's on 20th Street, two blocks from work.

This morning she is tired. She hasn't slept well. The streetlight outside her French doors shone in. She can't escape from the footsteps of people talking and walking by, or worse, from her own mind, which continues to create scenes, one more frightening than the next, of what is going on in her brother's head, right inside, so he can't run away.

She bolts upright, flips on the light and reaches for a cigarette. She sucks comfort deep into her lungs and begins to calm down, watching the smoke rise into the darkness overhead.

She remembers the fight she had with Jeremy over smoking when he was already sick. "What are you smoking for?" he demanded. "Why are you doing something to harm your own body?" He paced in front of his room, agitated. He slammed his fist into his closed door and it resounded throughout the house. He was almost in tears. "I'd give anything to be well and you're playing with your life!"

Now she watches the orange fire in the tip of her cigarette burn.

She visits him in the hospital, bringing her stories to give him hope, to entertain him. But her bravado is fading. She is exhausted.

Every night she tries to sleep, paces her wooden floor, lights cigarette after cigarette, in her own way keeping vigil with no energy to plan or dream, nothing but the rawness of her heart as she faces what life has become.

At the end where words fail, we will not go through the same door. But will you wait for me while I live my life? Will you stand in the doorway and wave to me? Will you turn and walk away, abandoning me here alone, my sweet, griping, pain-in-the-ass brother? Will I have to remember for the two of us—live for the two of us?

Sloan-Kettering Hospital, Manhattan—1993

CRUMBS

Packed and ready, Jeremy and I left for the hospital. I asked, on a scale of one to ten, how he was feeling. I knew it annoyed him but I couldn't help myself, as if I waited for his words to lower my anxiety. At one point, he shot back, "It's happening in my body, not yours!" I interpreted his words—leave me alone, or maybe, stop acting as if it's happening to you. It's not.

After the chemo, when he was settled in, I got up to leave. I had a new client and told Jeremy I would be back after work. All day, I found it hard to stay focused. I told my client that my son was sick, not the seriousness of it. I called a few times. He was asleep, then up vomiting.

We waited to see how his body would react to the second chemo treatment. They monitored his platelets. He couldn't go home until they were at a certain level.

The next day Jeremy called me at work. His voice trembled. "I'm scared, can you come see me?"

I arrived at the hospital with a hero sandwich for him. We walked to the rooftop play area. The city hummed around us. On this beautiful glorious September day, sunlight glinted off the tall buildings. The clear blue sky was free of summer's humidity with a crisp coolness that promised fall.

Backlit against the brilliant sky, he seemed pale and gaunt. I realized his vitality was gone. I watched my father die, and Jeremy looked like my father had at the end of his life. I reached over, took his hands in mine. We looked at each other with so much love, the rest of the world receded. We stayed like that for a long time.

We both knew the truth: he was dying. What courage it took to face this time! It wasn't that we denied the truth, the reality of it, but what could we really say and do? We could talk about the profound meaning beyond the words with simple gestures, simple talk.

So we savored that moment. We were together. Life was glorious, even then, even there. *Even there.*

He said, "When I get better, I want to...."

I knew this was the end. I looked at him, "Jeremy, don't wait until tomorrow. Live today. None of us knows how much time is left. We have this moment." I wanted to hold his face in my hands, to still his hesitant hoping. Not dash it, just refocus it, on there, then. To be grateful and in being grateful, to have it change from life's crumbs into something beautiful and holy because it was embraced in all its contradictions.

Jeremy no longer lay in his hospital bed waiting for his life to return to normal. He reached out for comfort, love, and hugs. Whatever he needed was there for him. The nurses loved him and vied for him to be part of their rounds. People visited, some were friends of our friends who came once to pay a visit and, enjoying his company, came back over and over. Containers of Chinese food, French fries, and spaghetti and meatballs were stacked on his tray. He laughed at his visitors' jokes, played cards, or watched TV. Maureen's fun-loving Aunt Peggy and Uncle Leo showed up with games and homemade food. Love flowed through Jeremy's eyes.

PARTY

THE NEXT TIME I SPENT THE NIGHT, JEREMY RENTED A MOVIE I WANTED to see called *Fire in the Sky*. After dinner he dialed the playroom, asking them to bring the movie. He looked comfortable in his environment and masterful, taking me to the movies. They brought the video and a tray of doughnuts, potato chips, popcorn, and cookies—enough for a party. He filled bowls and plates with as much as he wanted. At first I thought: *We'll never eat all this.* And then I thought: *So what?* He asked me to lie on the bed with him and the nurse found us holding hands, watching the movie with a bowl of popcorn between us. She joked with us—who would have thought we were in the pediatric cancer ward of a big hospital?

See, There He Is

By now I had known Tony less than nine months. I remembered how Paul abandoned me two weeks after Jeremy got sick. I couldn't go through that again. Why would a man whom I had known for such a short time take on such a burden? I decided to speak to him. "Tony, it's going to get very intense. If you don't want to go through Jeremy's death, let me know now. I couldn't handle you leaving me in the middle." He told me he wasn't going anywhere.

I knew his life wasn't easy. He had little money, less sleep. Yet he was present for me when I needed him. We would leave the hospital, race home to make passionate love. In the face of death, all we could do was affirm life.

Time was running out. Our lives consisted of tests, blood work, and medicine dosage adjustments. Jeremy developed diabetes from all the chemo, and the doctor taught me how to give him injections. I didn't want to stab a needle into my son's body. He said, "It's okay, Ma. It doesn't hurt."

The doctors tried to stabilize Jeremy so he could leave the hospital. At some point they decided to send him home and told him the good news. I was furious. I simply couldn't handle this alone; even with the few hours of nursing care each day that the insurance company allowed. I felt cornered. What if he had another massive seizure in the middle of the night? I grabbed the doctor and asked how he could tell him this without consulting me first. As a result Jeremy remained in the hospital where he could receive the medical care he needed even though he desperately wanted to go home.

Many nights I drove home exhausted. I remember one particular night when I woke up driving an unfamiliar road. I had fallen asleep at the wheel again and didn't know how long I'd been out. I vaguely remembered the Triborough Bridge, the Grand Central Parkway, then nothing. *Was I dreaming? Why was I in a car and not in bed?* I slowed down, tried to locate myself as I passed dark stores and houses. I stared at the shadowed road ahead of me, looking for a landmark. Then I saw the sign, Roslyn Road. I was almost home, but how I'd gotten there, I didn't know. Someone had guided my hands, kept me on the road and out of an accident.

Jenny didn't come often to the hospital to see her brother. He noticed, yet didn't say much except, "When's Jenny coming?" I knew it hurt him. He was at the end, and we all knew it. Every moment held too much for me to rush ahead with fears, what-ifs, or recriminations. I lived in the present where he was still alive, holding on to a lifesaver that protected me from the future.

When Jenny came to visit, I saw how thin she was, how much she used cigarettes and coffee as her lifeline to keep her going. *If she stopped, what then?*

I saw her brother, pale on white sheets. He was not going anywhere and he knew it. He was white, hairless, radiant in some way we others had not discovered. He asked me, "Will you just sit with me?" as I rushed around, keeping busy.

That was the hardest thing for me to do, because if I stopped, I would have to face that he was going and I was not.

See, There He Is

Sloan-Kettering Hospital, Manhattan—1993

TRUTH

A WORD FROM HIS DOCTOR WAS ENOUGH TO SEND OUR HOPES SOARING. The chemo was slowing down the cancer, or was that false hope? The delicate balance of his body tipped. They tried a new medication and his blood sugar shot up. Every solution hit the undeniable fact of his body breaking down. He was too sick to leave the hospital and his platelet count wasn't rising anymore. Yet the doctor talked about another operation, this one at Tisch Hospital, at NYU Medical Center, with Dr. E, a world-famous brain surgeon.

What was the truth? Something didn't make sense, and I needed to know what was best for Jeremy.

I took his MRIs, scans, and the doctor's letter to Dr. E because his office was near my work. I asked to speak with him and was told to come back later that day. I remember going to the cash machine on the street, sobbing uncontrollably.

Later in the day, Dr. E told me, straight out and right to the point, "Why are you going to subject him to this? He has maybe six months with the operation, six weeks to three months without it." I thanked him and walked to the elevator in shock, punched in the gut, and reeling. *So this was it!* I started to cry on the elevator and walked dazed into the street, knowing for certain that Jeremy was dying. I tried to hail a cab, while I screamed, doubled over. *Were people staring?* Somehow I got a cab to my car.

Somehow, how? I drove home and called Roger, my therapist. I hung onto the doorframe, screaming, waiting for him to answer.

The next day the doctors allowed me to take Jeremy home from Sloan for the night. I still worked with my new client, juggling the project and my extreme worry about Jeremy. My anxiety level soared off the map. Jeremy wanted corned beef for dinner. I drove to 86th Street in Manhattan, looking for a German butcher to buy the best for him. It was hot. It was late. I had just gotten my period and blood ran down my legs, but there was no time to deal with it. Jeremy wanted to escape to the safe haven of home. Every moment was precious, and I wanted to fill each one with as much life and love as possible.

We returned home, and he fell onto the couch. A large package of CDs from Columbia House had arrived. He was so sick he didn't even look at them. He lay there. I made dinner. Maureen and Jim came over to see him. Maureen noticed that our dog, Bonnie, was infested with fleas. She gave her a bath. I heard Bonnie barking in pain. I had no time to care for her so Maureen offered to take her home that night. We all had dinner together. Jeremy ate and ate and ate—his last meal at home.

He slept in my bed because I was afraid he might trip and hurt himself. He couldn't climb the stairs to his room anymore. I had work to finish but laid next to him on my bed, sleepless, listening to him breathe. In the morning he had an accident; he could no longer control his bowels. He was embarrassed, but I didn't care.

The memory of that last evening Jeremy was home is still vivid. Such drama—all of it set against the background of our peaceful haven. That night wasn't peaceful. It felt like a nightmare.

The next morning my client phoned, pressuring me. I called a friend to ask her what to do. I couldn't even think clearly. She told me to let the work go.

We drove to Sloan. Jeremy struggled; he didn't look good. As I negotiated Manhattan traffic, changing lanes and running red lights, he vomited into a plastic bag. They took him right into a hospital room for tests. I was hysterical, shaking at the front desk of the pediatric ward, screaming that I couldn't handle it anymore. The social worker calmly took the work from me, along with my client's name and address, and relieved me of the whole project.

IGNORE

Despite my misgivings, the doctors decided to put Jeremy into Tisch Hospital for surgery. We didn't want to give up hope yet. I called Tony from Sloan and asked him to come. Meanwhile Vinny arrived and we took Jeremy by cab to the medical center.

When we arrived at Tisch, they admitted him, and he had dinner in his room. The doctors were celebrating Rosh Hashanah, yet they determined by phone what Jeremy's physical state was and what was best for him. The operation was scheduled for Monday. I wondered why Dr. E had agreed to operate after what he told me.

The nurses gave Jeremy medication to help him sleep. I went down to the cafeteria and found Tony wandering the halls. He had visited two hospitals searching for us. And there he was, a blessing.

The next morning when I spoke with Vinny at his house, he told me that Jeremy was running a fever and the nurses wanted him sent back to Sloan. He was too sick for them to care for. *What?* I immediately called Tisch and asked questions. Were they giving him medication for his fever? *No.* When did it start? *Early this morning.* And you just let him lie there? *Yes.*

I was furious and needed answers. I presumed all hospitals gave the care we were used to at Sloan.

Tony and I raced into Manhattan and up to Jeremy's ward. He was screaming for the nurse, in pain, half in and half out of the bed. He needed the bathroom, but because he was hooked to a stationary IV, he couldn't move. His roommate said he'd been calling for a nurse for a long time. No one had come.

The nurse's station was empty. I ran to the other rooms. No nurses. Patients moaned and called out. I finally found one, grabbed her and screamed, "Where are all the nurses? My son needs help!"

Suddenly, five nurses materialized. I demanded that they take care of my son. Why hadn't he been given medication for his fever? Why had no one called us? What was his temperature? Was he getting his other medications?

They knew he was dying and didn't provide care for him. He might have been just another sick patient to them, but he was my son.

Jeremy became hysterical. The head nurse pulled me into the hall and said, "You're setting him off, calm down. He's reacting to your feelings." I screamed through tears, "He's dying, how could you treat him like this?" Then I decided to phone for an ambulance to take him back to Sloan.

The ambulance attendants placed Jeremy on a gurney. He looked at me, weak and exhausted. I said, "You will never go through anything like this again. I promise you."

Tony and I rode the elevator with Jeremy. I covered his face to protect him from the rain as we climbed into the ambulance for the drive to Sloan.

When we arrived, the elevator opened on the eighth floor and the nurses waited. "Hi, Jeremy. Welcome back." They moved into action. Tony commented, "What a difference." We were back in their loving arms.

The nurses settled Jeremy, and I watched him sleep, unwilling to leave the hospital. I turned on the TV; *Groundhog Day* was playing. Over and over Bill Murray's character woke at seven to the sound of Sonny & Cher singing "I Got You Babe." He had endless chances to get the day right, to grow kinder, to finally learn how to love.

ALL PRETENSE OF WORKING CEASED. JEREMY ASKED ME TO SPEND MORE time with him. I kept busy in his room, brought him juice, cleaned up, and talked to the nurses and doctors. I didn't know what to do with my emotions; I used motion to diffuse them. I couldn't sit still.

I asked my friend and masseuse, Claudie, to come once a week to massage Jeremy. She refused to take payment, asking only for carfare. For five Sundays she commuted by bus from Yonkers. The nurses drew the curtains and Claudie worked on Jeremy. He loved it. Claudie taught me how to feel Jeremy's energy field and how to comb it to soothe him. She showed me how to massage his feet, which also calmed him.

The counselor at Sloan told me that Jeremy and I were a good team. I lent him my courage and strength and contributed to his doing so well.

I brought flowers and hanging plants into Jeremy's room. Roger gave me a photo of a beautiful fall tree with red leaves. He said life burns the brightest right before it goes out. He also gave me pictures of beautiful women to tack on his wall.

As far as I heard, Jeremy made no comment about the pictures, but when Vinny came into his room, he was upset and asked who put up the photos. His view was why taunt him with what he can't have.

One evening Jeremy urged me to attend my monthly women's art group, something I had missed for several months. I hadn't wanted to leave Jeremy but he insisted. It was my turn for the other women artists to critique my drawings and paintings in their Long Island City loft. Maybe the others were comfortable showing their work. However, the experience was still new to me.

That small visit to my everyday life felt surreal. I could leave yet Jeremy couldn't. His world had closed down to a hospital room, an IV dripping into his black and blue veins.

HER

A pen waits on his hospital bed, black against the white sheet, waiting to become part of the unfolding story. Should he sign his name on the line that says yes? He waits for her to come and that knowledge comforts him as he sits alone with the lights dimmed for the night. He holds on to her, imagines that she is close by. Maybe she is even rising up now in the elevator, shouldering her bag and coming like an angel of mercy, as she has come so many other times to help him carry this load.

She arrives every day bringing home with her: the lazy afternoons on the porch, the food cooked in the kitchen, the safety her smile represents. He can hear the traffic from eight floors below, the roar even at this hour. She doesn't know what he will tell her, but he knows he can trust her, he knows she will not fail him.

Beside the pen lay the forms, the official story of the way his life has veered off track. She is his last hope. Her face will speak before her lips even part. They will be strong, they will continue on because there is no going back.

He remembers how years ago they used to sing those silly songs while she rocked him in the rocking chair, even though he was really too old for it.

SIGN

When I returned at ten to the dimmed lights of the pediatric ward, Jeremy was still awake and had papers on the bed in front of him. I queried him with my eyes.

"The doctor brought in a do-not-resuscitate order for me to fill out."

He looked at me with the question in his eyes. He wanted to fight on, and I knew it was over. I rummaged around in my mind for a response but had none. I sat quiet, with this new development, not surprised but stunned nevertheless. What truth could I give him that would honor the choice in front of us? Not a place either of us wanted to be but ours nevertheless. This was not the time for glib reassurances or easy phrases that roll off the tongue, thrown out to push away the fear. The starkness. "Jeremy," I finally said, "I would want to live or die. I wouldn't want to exist in limbo, in a coma. I don't know what's on the other side. I'm scared, but I know Poppy is there."

He and I had both felt my father's presence around us since the middle of September. He told me Poppy was around him a lot now. I asked how that felt. He said, "Like I'm wrapped in a warm blanket."

We sat together, he propped up in bed, I in the hospital side chair in the low-lit room. I wanted to take him away from this. We sat in silence. Finally he looked up and asked me for the pen. I reached over and handed it to him. He pulled the paper towards him and signed.

See, There He Is

Sloan-Kettering Hospital, Manhattan—1993

EDDY

Sloan-Kettering occupies the lower edge of hospital row, a few blocks from Hunter College and some of my happiest years. I gazed at the 59th Street Bridge from the eighth floor window of the pediatric oncology ward. Small bald children walked the floor with plasma drips or blood bags attached into their veins. Acting like kids, some climbed on the metal wheels of the stands that held the bags and rolled through the halls. Some simply lay in bed.

Parents were always around. In the communal kitchen's refrigerator, we placed labeled containers with our children's foods and treats. The nurses' station was nearby and all night its lights shone as we got up to tend to our children. I met other mothers washing dishes or doing laundry late at night. We shared our stories and traded advice. This family of mothers, thrown together by our children's cancer, was a comfort. I met mothers from the Middle East, from expensive suburban towns in Connecticut, from neighborhoods in the Bronx and Queens; black, Hispanic, white, rich, and poor, all of us prayed, making bargains with our various Gods—Allah, Jesus, Yahweh. We slept in recliners or propped up on two chairs, a nightmarish rest where morning felt like a hangover. We stared down at people walking to work, delivery trucks with handcarts, or taxis with their red lights in a row funneling workers southward. We watched a picture of the world we vaguely remembered. And as we glanced back, our children lay, bald-headed and pale on white sheets with saline drips and needles in their veins; bedpans, water pitchers, and curtains suggesting an unobtainable privacy from the family beside the next bed, who mirrored our early morning.

I heard the roar of the city beneath me rising up from the street. Horns honked and planes grazed the low clouds. I got up exhausted and refilled Jeremy's glass with fresh water, greeted the nurse, gentle loving angel who worked there among the children.

There was caring and love, yet the news was harsh. There was no going back. We had examined this alley for a way out but found none. His platelets were at twenty-five, dangerously low. No more rounds of chemo were planned; no more poison in hopes of killing the killer inside Jeremy before it killed him. His body was strong; the cancer was stronger. The delicate balance had been tipped. I called on God's various names, looking for hope. There was none. Hope was the last thing to die before the reality of death took hold.

Dawn's red glow streaked over Manhattan. I stood there loving my son, tending to his needs. He didn't want to be a burden. We still believed in miracles.

I TOOK PICTURES OF HIM SO A PSYCHIC COULD TELL ME WHAT SHE SAW. After he died, I stared at the photos. He already knew the truth. He knew where this would go. In the photo, he stared at me, one eye and side of his face screwed up—that was the cancer doing that. He was bald and beautiful in his realness—a spiritual quality. He was only partly there, the door was open and he was close to the other side.

GAZING AT THESE PICTURES ALL THESE YEARS LATER, I SEE MY SON IN his St. John's T-shirt. His eyes hold so much emotion that at first I turn away. It's too much to bear. Trapped in the bed. Weary. Resigned. I look at him and have an almost uncontrollable desire to reach into the picture and save him from his fate. I think of all the fun we had, of his playful spirit, how eager he was to join in.

WATCHING

I OPENED THE FRONT DOOR AND THREW DOWN MY BAG AND PACKAGES, glad to have my arms free. I wasn't alone. It happened yesterday too. I looked behind the door to my left because that's where I was drawn. Nothing. *Was it the grief, the knowing that he was dying? Was that throwing me off so the world looked odd?* Nothing seemed solid. No, my impression was that someone was behind the door, waiting. I was comforted.

Who was there? He seemed to stand there alert, poised to be of help. I felt his concern, his love. I remember visiting my mother in the nursing home and feeling my father's presence by the window watching over her. Watching me. People might think me crazy, but I knew it was my father.

Yes, my father waited for me behind the door every time I came home. Yes, it had to be him—not saying anything, slightly anxious, letting me know I wasn't alone. He had come for Jeremy. I was past believing Jeremy would live and drew comfort from knowing my father, his beloved Poppy, would be there when he crossed over. Many things not of this material world had happened over the last two years. They had made me a believer. How many times when I was about to fall, did a stranger reach for me as I stumbled? They watched over me through physical acts with physical people so I couldn't dismiss them. These were no coincidences. I called for help, begged for it, and it came.

WITNESS

My father loved more than anything to take us into the woods every weekend. We lived in a one-bedroom apartment in the Bronx, but unlike many of our neighbors, we had a car. He loaded us up in the early morning. In those days before the New York State Thruway was built, we drove Westchester's country roads back to the place he called home—the woods.

It took until my forties to find Lincolndale, the Catholic orphanage he was raised in, now a home for wayward boys. He'd never showed us where he lived. When we were young, he brought my brother and me to Silver Lake, the Croton Reservoir, Anthony Wayne State Park, and the Hudson River on picnics and walks, instilling in us without a word his love of nature and the wild. We swam and splashed. I can see him now, smiling his toothy grin, the worry lines on his forehead smoothed out as he gave us what he didn't have.

My father was a solitary man. His eyes, like the tip of an iceberg, hinted at the many stories he had never told.

There he is, turning burgers on the grill while my mother cuts up juicy red Jersey tomatoes. There he is, with his ever-present camera, freezing us into memories he could hold and smile at later.

His fear hung around him, passed on to us, the children ready to jump off the raft into deep water. The joy of childhood abandon.

I hope we gave him back some of what he never received. I hope we healed his heart. I remain a witness to his silent life. He taught me to understand what wasn't being said, although at the time I hated him. His son, my brother, Jim, left as soon as he could, and didn't look back.

Vinny, Kyle, and I took turns staying at the hospital. Vinny arrived with his overnight bag to relieve me. I updated him, kissed Jeremy and turned to leave. Vinny stood on the other side of Jeremy's bed. "Poor kid," he said. "I wish I could take this away. I wish I had cancer instead of him."

At the time, I couldn't hear the sincerity of his words. He held his emotions tightly in check, and I didn't understand.

I went home to shower, eat if I could, care for our parakeets, Perry and Cecil, and gather things to bring back. I was not living in the world; I only visited it from my post on the eighth floor.

The red maple outside our home was gorgeous and dropping leaves, the ground was covered with them. Leaves lay calf deep on my pathway. I pushed through them, climbed the steps to the beautiful porch, our sanctuary. I could not stay. I was only passing through.

As I showered, I was shocked to see that my body was healthy. I stared in disbelief as the water ran down my face.

One early Saturday morning in mid October after about three weeks in the hospital, Jeremy called; he sounded very frightened. He asked me to come right away. I calmed him down and told him I would be there later in the morning, then went back to sleep, something I regretted for years to come.

Two hours later one of the nurses called to inform me that Jeremy had a massive seizure and was in an agitated state. I jumped up, got dressed and Tony and I raced into Manhattan. How could I have ignored him when he begged me to come right away?

Jeremy screamed. Tossed. I had never seen him so upset. They moved his roommate out because Jeremy's screams terrified him. Jeremy was fighting. They sedated him. Vinny arrived from his home. When Jeremy woke up, he was agitated and yelled at us. At first we couldn't understand what was the matter. Every time we talked to him, he screamed, "I can't hear you! What are you saying?" Finally we wrote our questions on a small pad and he answered, saying there was a loud buzzing in his ears. Small slips of paper allowed us to reconnect.

SLIPS

Platelet count yesterday 36. Dilantin level 15. Both good.
It's night.
I'm staying tonight.
Try to sleep for a little bit.
This is some medicine to relax you.
I will not let them hurt you.
Smaller pieces of chicken?
Tell Jenny what?
We'll have Thanksgiving dinner soon. Who do you want to invite?
I'm getting the juice for you.
I love you.
The chemo did it.
We think your hearing will get better.
I will be with you.
We'll try everything.

Look at me. You are very sick.
I can't make you better.
The cancer is growing.
You will not be in pain.

COMA

JEREMY BEGAN TO CALM DOWN. THE DOCTOR MOVED HIM TO A PRIVATE room at the end of the ward because he was dying, so that the other children would not witness this.

Exhausted, Jeremy slept the rest of the day and through the night. I wondered if he would wake up. That night I stayed in his room, listened to him toss and moan, talking in his sleep. I didn't understand all of what he was saying, but knew he was not at peace. I didn't want him lost in a coma—roaming through the unconscious world with no voice to guide him. Many times that night, I woke to soothe him, rub his back, and whisper comforting words.

I wasn't experiencing the slow deterioration of my body, trapped with ringing in my ears, everyone existing outside my fading senses. I decided to tell him he was dying, even though I realized he must know. Maybe if he heard the words, he would find peace.

Early the next morning, I told Dr. Thompson that Jeremy needed to know the truth when he woke, no more pep talks or false hopes.

All along, he'd clung to the belief that if he took his medicines and passed his neurological tests, he would win. He was supported by the strength of our collective love. Now I delivered the dreaded words, "You are going to die," dashing his hope. If I spoke the truth, I feared it would cause him to die.

"It's over, Jeremy." I said as I held his hand. "We've fought and done everything possible and it's not working. It's not working! It's not enough."

He didn't say anything at first. I could see he heard me. I felt I had let him down, maybe even lied to his trusting young heart. Although

Jeremy was groggy, he asked for everyone he loved to come. I phoned, saying, "It's time." His paternal grandparents had arrived from Florida already. Sean's sister, Shannon, flew back from France; Sean came down from college in Maine.

I love you so much, but I can't save you. I can only tell you the truth and show you the way out. Leave as fast as you can! There's no need to linger. Go! Go! Go! Don't look back. It will only get worse. Yet all I could say was: Leave. Don't suffer.

The next afternoon, he woke again. His father, grandparents, Maureen and Jim and others greeted him.

He gave me a confused look and said, "I'm not dead yet! I'm still strong." He seemed annoyed that I told him he was dying, as if my words were part of a bad dream.

I sighed and took his hand in mine. "Jeremy, your soul and spirit are very strong, that will never change, but your body is very sick. It's not going to get better." I stopped to give my words time to sink in. At first he didn't say anything. "You will be safe, I promise you. Poppy is waiting for you. I love you. We all love you. It's okay to let go and leave."

I could feel his anger and sadness.

He looked at me. "I feel ripped off."

"It sucks, Jeremy. You have been ripped off."

I felt such infinite love and tenderness, saying goodbye to him. We had struggled so. He said, "I love you SO much, Mom." I'm sure he watched the drama going on around him—everyone dealing with their emotions as best they could as he looked at us.

The next day he woke in the afternoon, again surrounded by friends and relatives. We talked for a while and then he looked at me and asked, "How are you doing?"

"I'm okay. Don't worry about me."

He looked past me and asked, "Who's that standing behind you?"

Tony replied, "It's Tony."

He asked Tony, "How is she doing?"

"Your mother is doing okay."

He drifted more and more into a coma. It seemed that after these conversations, he did let go. Friends and family visited him every day. He asked and they showed up—crying, laughing, eating, massaging his feet, kissing him, and stroking his comatose body. We worked together like one organism, focused on supporting him on his journey. Vinny's brothers and sisters came; my friends came to support me. Every night, Vinny, Kyle, or I stayed. He was not left alone. He lay there relaxed and peaceful. I know he felt our love and support in that last week. I believe it made his transition easier.

Whenever I returned to his room, I leaned over, took his hand and whispered, "Hi Jeremy. It's Mom." He moaned. I put a cool facecloth on his hot forehead. "I love you, Jeremy. Let go and go to the light. Remember, just look for the light, honey."

Tony had given me a book about how to help loved ones die and the image of going to the light felt very powerful. People who had near-death experiences talked about the tunnel that led to the light, and the guides who awaited them.

We told the doctors we wanted no measures used to extend his life. The doctor in charge of the floor didn't agree. They held a conference and brought in a new doctor who supported our decision. Jeremy was taken to surgery and an IV implanted in his neck so that he could continue to receive his pain medication and fluids intravenously. His black and blue arms were finally free of tubes.

We stood watch. Sometimes fifteen to twenty people crowded into his room, spilling into the hallways outside. We shared food, took turns with whatever chores needed doing, and comforted each other.

I bought a camera. At first I wondered if it was a good idea. I left it on the dresser, and visitors took photos of him and of each other—a record of his last days:

— Vinny and I leaned over Jeremy, my hand on his heart while he received the last rites.

— Jenny held his hand, her face lost in sadness.

— Maureen and Kyle wiped his forehead.

— Tony smiled up at me from a chair in his red sweatshirt.

— Vinny's brother, Fulton, and sister, Bernadette, talked quietly by the door.

I hold a photograph from that last week as I look back over the memories. Someone had taken a close-up picture of Vinny, Jeremy, and me. I reach in from the left, wearing a yellow sweater, wiping Jeremy's face with a cool cloth. Vinny leans in from the right, wearing a blue striped shirt. Our heads almost touch, framing Jeremy who lay there pale, with a swollen face. He doesn't look like my beautiful son anymore. Vinny holds Jeremy's hand, whispering to him, and although he is in a coma, Jeremy's eyes are open, turned to his father. I wonder if he hears his father's words?

WAIT

A few days before Jeremy dies, two of Vinny and Kyle's friends, Donna and Ronnie, are at Jeremy's bedside when Tony and I arrive. Donna suggests we give him a bath. I hesitate, but she is a nurse and takes charge, getting towels, bowls, soap, and lotion. We stand by his bed; they on one side, Tony and I on the other. Donna takes off Jeremy's T-shirt and we, following her cue, begin to wash him. He is thin, bone thin. There is a rhythm to our movements. I think of mothers throughout time washing their dead, honoring them.

We wet the facecloth, pour on soap and wash his right arm, rinse the cloth and wipe him clean with a soft white towel. Donna shows us how to help her turn him over. His hips and ribs stand out against his wasted flesh. We are silent, taking in his body, lying there quiet. No one talks. We rub lotion onto his skin, massaging and soothing him. Tending his body. I massage his feet, each heel has a huge blister from lying in bed for so long. I remember that before he lapsed into a coma he asked us to rub his feet. How it soothed him. Does he feel our hands touching him, our tender motions. Our slow respectful journey?

A nurse comes in to tell us she gave him a bath earlier. We look at her, and turn back to our work. I gather fresh clothes to dress him in. No matter how much I wash them, they still smell of chemicals, acrid and strong. Jeremy's scent is gone.

I felt helpless at the time, watching Jeremy die. Although I didn't have a chance to wash him after he died, I look back and remember the four of us in that silent room, honoring my son, letting him feel the love coming through our hands, and I am comforted.

There is nothing left to do but wait. I don't remember much except the flow of people in and out during that last week. The days and nights blend one into the other, night becomes day, day fades into night. *What did I eat? Did I eat? When did I go home?*

I have a memory of Tony driving my friend and me home one night. We start laughing over something and can't stop; we laugh without control, from deep inside. Whenever we look at each other, we erupt into fresh howls until tears run down our faces. At first it seems disrespectful to be laughing. But then nothing seems odd anymore, seems other than what it is—in the moment, crossing 96th Street heading for the FDR Drive, the Triborough Bridge, and home.

Sloan-Kettering, Manhattan—October 28, 1993

BREATH

The last rays of the setting sun shine golden through the hospital window and fall on Jeremy, as we surround his bed, ten of us. Soon to be nine.

The room is silent, so silent we can hear his in-breaths and out-breaths, which come deep and steady.

Every time he lets out his breath, I hold mine, waiting for him to suck air into his lungs. As if it would make a difference!

We are here to witness his last hours, all of us quiet because this hospital room feels like a church, and we are reverent yet unsure of how his dying will go.

I think this is the first time each of us witnesses a loved one's death. And not just anyone but the one we had strived to keep alive, each in our own way.

I sit in a chair beside the bed holding my son's right hand with my left hand placed on his heart. I wait for the struggle, fear it, but it doesn't come. In a coma, he doesn't fight anymore. He has given over this part of his journey to his body.

Our nurse, Laura, enters and with hardly a sound checks his vital signs. I look at her and she nods. Laura is one of Jeremy's favorite nurses. Many of them clamor to care for him at the end.

Jenny rushes to the door and slips out of the room. I hear her going, "Jen…" I call out, but don't move.

His breaths become more measured now, as if he is testing the space between here and there. Each one seems deliberate, chosen. Swinging between life and death like a pendulum.

His face is pale. His cheeks fiery. Fevered. I sense the battle inside his body. His chest is warm under my hand.

We do not speak.

His breath becomes slower now, each in-breath held, maybe gathering momentum to propel him to the other side: a leap he is getting ready to make.

He breathes out, then there is a pause, which goes on for some time and finally, another in-breath.

I let my breath out.

Finally he breathes out and we wait for the next in-breath. It does not come. He is quiet. We call for the doctor and he checks for vital signs. There are none. It is 6:56 p.m., October 28, 1993. Jeremy's face is at rest. His eye no longer scrunches up with tension. He again looks like my son, mouth slightly open, asleep.

I look at his nose sprinkled with freckles, his now-smooth brow. I lean over and kiss his face. He has let go; his face no longer flushed. He is gone. I begin to wail. Vinny reaches over and pulls me toward the door. Out into the hallway.

"Get a hold of yourself!" he says. I am too shocked to protest or answer back. I stand there, taking deep breaths until I calm down. We go back in.

How pale Jeremy is, like porcelain; all the color in his face—the redness of life—has drained away. I stare at the whiteness of his skin.

Vinny, Jim, and others empty out his drawers and the bedside table, fill shopping bags with his clothes and belongings. The movement swirls around me as I stare at my son.

I feel myself ushered out, unable to protest. I want to stay and sit with him. I want to be silent, to love his dead body. Yet I am leaving. We are all leaving and Jeremy remains. I turn to look at him.

Jenny waits in the hallway with her boyfriend, leaning against the wall, her arms wrapped around herself. She is pale and shaking. I put my arms around her and ask if she wants to come home with me, but she wants to go to her apartment. I can't bear the idea of her being alone tonight. I need her close, so she won't disappear too. She insists she'd rather be home tonight. I turn to her boyfriend and ask him to please go with her, to not let her go home alone. He hesitates and I repeat my words. He looks at me and nods.

PART II
1993-1995

Sea Cliff—1993

EMPTIED

Tony and I drove back to Sea Cliff. The leaves piled on my walkway crunch as we pushed through them. We lugged shopping bags filled with Jeremy's clothes up the front steps. The house was quiet. I wandered around, then up to Jeremy's room. I picked the stuffed pig up, remembering how we played with it. Nothing made sense, and I was too exhausted to think about it.

I watched him be born and I watched him die. These words ran through my head as I woke. I had agreed to let the hospital remove his brain for research, something that to this day I regret. I imagined his sweet face and thought of his head being emptied and could go no further—one more desecration. I knew they were trying to help others, but didn't he give enough already?

Vinny, Kyle, and I went to the local funeral home across the street from the nursery where Jeremy and I used to buy Christmas ornaments and chocolate chip cookies. We ordered a plain wooden coffin because we felt this best suited him. I noticed the funeral transport car in the driveway as we left, and wondered if Jeremy's body was in it. I stopped at the local florist to order flowers—big yellow sunflowers, orange, red and purple flowers—a grave blanket filled with the colors of life.

I gathered Jeremy's pants and the purple silk shirt we had bought last Christmas not imagining they would be his burial clothes, along with soft moccasins and his favorite baseball cap.

I didn't know if I had the strength to face the next three days prior to his funeral. There was activity everywhere; it swirled around me as I floated like a leaf in the unstoppable current.

My friends Esther and Ed arrived that afternoon and took Tony and me out to dinner. I leaned on her, remembering how devastated she was after her son died. She had survived and I needed her strength.

Each day people came to pay their respects—all our relatives and friends, Vinny's, Jenny's, and mine—and Jeremy's friends. The room was filled with people; I could hardly walk through. Sean and I stared at Jeremy in his coffin. I gave him one of Jeremy's baseball caps. I wanted all his friends to have something of his.

We gathered photos of Jeremy's life, and they filled a large illustration board:

—Jeremy as a little boy

—Jeremy, Jenny, and I huddled close together, smiling for a Polaroid as we started life after I left Vinny

—Jeremy mugged for the camera in his yellow "Save the Whales" T-shirt with sweat-plastered hair, those big freckles, and his tongue sticking out between two missing front teeth

—Jeremy held the horseback-riding medal he won at the dude ranch

—Jeremy at his junior high school graduation, tall and handsome in his red robes, looking solemn, his dark hair perfectly groomed

—Jeremy and Sean, good buddies, lounged comfortably with each other

I wanted everyone to see how normal my beautiful son looked before cancer wiped his life away. My mother's three sisters, Ceil, Mary, and Helen, from Bayonne sat in chairs at the back talking with my cousins Rosemary and Mike. I was in constant motion, answering questions, being introduced to Vinny's friends, standing with Tony who was dressed in a suit, something I had never seen him in before. Jenny talked to her cousins beside the pictures of Jeremy.

PLOD

Monday, November 1, All Souls Day, was the morning of Jeremy's funeral at Fordham University Chapel. Tony, Jenny, and I visited him at the funeral home. I gazed at his body in the coffin for the last time, kissed his cold cheek. Our sweet life and memories, and his funny loving spirit were gone.

The funeral was no comfort to me—each of us trapped in the prison of our own shattered hearts. We followed the coffin. Six of our friends struggled under its weight. Sean, at the far end, carried his friend down the concrete path and up the church steps. The bells tolled and the cold November wind blew leaves across our path. We plodded, or was there a word for the need to move forward while wanting to turn back? We were attached to the back of the coffin. It pulled us into the church. Upright, we walked slowly.

Vinny was tall, gray, and somber. Jenny was dressed in a tight black suit buttoned to her neck, her wild hair wrapped primly in a bun. Her face looked liquid and ripe.

The ritual—a Catholic mass—the word-numbing sermon and endless prayers as I waited from years of habit, watching the white satin-draped coffin float in a cloud of incense. When would all this be over? I glanced the length of the coffin, imagined Jeremy lying inside. My beloved family, with our years of disputes, angers, tenderness, and broken hearts, all mourned together.

Yet no one touched. We bumped against each other, already checked out.

I sensed the feelings written on our faces years later while watching the video my brother-in-law filmed of the mass. It was like looking at ghosts, a former Jenny, Vinny, Tony, Maureen, Jim, Sean, and me. This video weighed a thousand tons. I could hardly move, felt sick and disoriented from watching its flickering images.

I saw that no one touched and I grieved for our inability to dissolve into each other's arms. There was no comfort and maybe even then we knew nothing could save us. We were on fire and could not be put out. As the priest droned on, I strained to hear something relevant to my son, but grew weary and fast forwarded; I didn't hear the words the first time either.

A distant God in an echoing church brought me no comfort. I was still polite, the good girl following the rules. I honored others' beliefs, but I wanted this day over.

Tony held me up. We sleepwalked in slow motion from the church, played our entry in reverse. The bagpipe droned, off-key. "*Amazing grace. How sweet it is,*" when nothing felt sweet. The bagpipe sounded like an animal being strangled.

HE WAS BURIED AT GATE OF HEAVEN CEMETERY IN VALHALLA, NEW York, in his grandparents' plot, under three huge pine trees. They towered over us, shading the grave. Dried leaves blew in the bitter cold wind, chilling every inch of bare skin.

THE DAY AFTER JEREMY DIED, I CALLED MY BROTHER JIM. HE WAS IN Japan on business. He called me when he returned a few days later, and when I told him Jeremy was dead, he put his wife, Lynn, on the phone. Listening to my story, she said, "That's interesting." *Interesting?* I thought. Devastating was a word that came to my mind. Not interesting. She handed the phone back to Jim and we hung up, promising to call so we could reconnect. That didn't happen.

I FELT AS IF I HAD BEEN ILL AND NEEDED TO REST. I SLEPT ON AND OFF for a week, maybe two. Tony stayed with me most of the time. I don't remember if he went to work. I don't remember if I saw Jenny or not. I ate food put in front of me, ravenous, although I said over and over, "I'm not hungry," while stuffing food into my mouth. "Take human bites," Tony said.

The week after Jeremy's death, I drove back to Gate of Heaven Cemetery just to be sure I could find his grave. First I stopped at a nursery and bought a little pumpkin, the kind we decorated each Halloween with funny faces. I drove through the tall iron gates watched over by two stone angels. The road curved through the mausoleums. I turned left, before realizing I had to go down the hill.

Up ahead I saw three pine trees and knew I was close to his grave. I knelt down and placed the pumpkin on his gravestone for my little boy.

Deerfield Beach, Florida—1993

BEACH

Esther and Ed invited Jenny and me to Florida for Thanksgiving, best to be far away on this first holiday without Jeremy. They knew what we faced and didn't try to cheer us up. They provided dinners, pool, talk when needed, and quiet when exhaustion washed over us. Jenny read one of Esther's novels, curled up on the couch. We spent Thanksgiving Day on the beach in warm Florida sunshine, unlike the cold blustery New York version we were used to. That evening we went out for Thanksgiving dinner. Esther didn't cook much and neither Jenny nor I could bear preparing the foods Jeremy loved.

The following morning we borrowed Esther's car and drove to the beach, where we bought strong coffee. We sat on the curb watching the surf roll in, and received whatever small comfort we could from this nearness. We were the shocked survivors.

On the way home, waiting in a check-in line at the airport, I told the woman behind me that my son had just died. Her reaction was to tear up and say, "How terrible!" No longer at the hospital, I was alone with my thoughts although I was still numb to my feelings.

I didn't know what to make of this place where I had landed, with too much empty time.

Back at La Guardia Airport, Jenny took a cab to Manhattan. Last year, when I visited Esther before Jeremy's last operation, Jeremy picked me up, looking pale, carrying my winter coat over his arm. I stared past the limo drivers holding up signs for arriving passengers. No Jeremy. I hadn't made preparations to get home. Tony's beeper didn't answer. I called a car service.

I watched the Cross Island Parkway and the Long Island Expressway speed by until we turned onto Shore Road, then up Sea Cliff Avenue into my beloved town. The van stopped at my dark house. I stepped out.

Sea Cliff—1993

VOYEUR

By early December, I needed to return to work and called Oscar. I had turned my back on him and expected him to hang up. I said, "Hi Oscar," and his response was, "When are you coming back?"

The familiar routine of work at the ad agency and my three-hour round-trip daily commute into Manhattan kept me grounded in life.

Every day I woke with my heart leaden inside me. My arms and legs didn't seem to be connected to anything, didn't work together anymore. Every muscle in my body hurt. Walking entailed dragging my body forward, lurching with the effort. *Would I fall? Did I care?* I needed to get up, eat food I didn't taste, lock the door, and get into my Honda for the drive to Manhattan on automatic pilot. I merged with the day, not caring what it brought. *What was the point?*

I triple-checked my work, afraid of making mistakes. My mind felt encased in thick cotton and it frustrated me.

Every night I left work, turned the corner on Fifth Avenue and Seventeenth Street and at the parking lot, entered my safe haven—the car. The pent-up emotion carried all day poured out in sobs and wails as I drove the streets of Manhattan towards the Queens Midtown Tunnel and home.

I was relieved to return to my grief, to take my mask off. I'd heard how women keened for their dead and now knew what that felt like. It was primal. No teacher other than death could show me the way. I wailed and keened all the way home. *How had my body held all this in for so many hours?*

Then I reached Sea Cliff and the familiar empty rooms. Bonnie came to greet me.

I thought back to when I decided to move to Sea Cliff. Jeremy started badgering me about getting cable. Bayside wasn't hooked up yet. The only reason he packed up his room and moved was the promise of cable service on the other end.

The cable guy drove up two days after we moved in and Jeremy hovered, making sure he installed it right. Before the guy even left, Jeremy found the Comedy Channel, Eddie Murphy, and *Caddy Shack*. Taped shows began filling his shelf. I heard him laugh. *This is good*, I thought.

In Living Color with Damon Wayans as the homeless man carrying around a jar filled with a floating brown object sent us into breathless hysterics. Jim Carrey, as Fireman Bill, twisting his body into impossible shapes, took us places nothing else could.

Most nights Jeremy and I lay on his bed, laughing through one show after another. When he wasn't watching the Comedy Channel or Giants football, he rented every comedy video from the local store. If laughter was the best medicine, he took double doses.

We both knew the facts—the weekly trips to Sloan-Kettering, the drugs and operations. What was he supposed to do? Some might call it escapism; we didn't give a damn.

After he died, I returned the cable box to the company. I couldn't laugh anymore. It wouldn't come unplugged. I pulled and shook it, finally beat it with a hammer until the box shattered, its insides hanging out. I had no idea what to tell the cable company. I gathered the pieces into a box and left it on the front porch for their pickup. When I returned home, it was gone.

No one ever called to ask what happened. I received no bill for damages. His room was quiet, and echoed while I sorted through his clothes, books, and videos, gathering everything into piles. Nothing was being thrown out. One pile was for TC, his half-brother. Jenny wanted his mattress and some of his clothes.

I searched for secrets to his inner life. I pored through school notebooks, pages of arithmetic homework, and an essay written about his illness, very matter of fact though. I hadn't asked the questions I now wanted answers to, like "Were you afraid to die?" or "Did you feel lonely?"

Did he ever make love? I started to say have sex, but that seemed so callous. Okay, make love. Not that he would talk about it to his mother.

I went through his wallet. It contained his driver's license, credit card, health insurance card, a five-dollar bill, receipts from the drug store, and appointment cards from the hospital. I was sad to see the focus, at nineteen, on his illness. I looked for secret pockets, phone numbers, anything, all the while feeling strange about the trespass. *What's this?* In a small slit, I felt something and pulled out a condom. *Why was it important that my son experienced that human ecstasy?* I wanted it for him. So much else had been taken away.

I asked Jenny years later if he had been a virgin. She didn't know. She suggested asking his best friend, Sean, but I couldn't—that felt like an intrusive mother question. *What did it matter?* It was too late now.

I sorted through all his things: a voyeur into his life. Maybe that's why he left no record. He valued his privacy and he had to know I would look. I found cards from his friends, letters to the girl he liked. He had gotten tickets to *Phantom of the Opera*; then she was unable to go because she was out of town with her parents. She seemed sweet but had no idea there would be no other chance for him. I was left to reconstruct his inner world from a few boxes of flotsam and jetsam tossed up on shore.

He did share his feelings as much as he could, and he was only nineteen. *Did I expect too much?* I thought of myself at nineteen, all over the place.

I discovered that Jeremy had confided in his sister. She told me his fears as she began to heal. "Why is this happening to me?" "I'm afraid of dying." It was a lot for her to carry, and for that I grieved.

So much hope had brought Jeremy and me to that old drafty cottage in Sea Cliff. Now the walls suffocated me. I bolted out of the empty house every night just to reassure myself that life continued. 1993-1994 was the coldest winter I remember and snow piled up everywhere. The streets became slippery when they refroze after dark. I wandered Dubois Street down Littleworth Lane, past lighted windows and families eating dinner, feeding on their lives.

Sometimes I walked Main Street or Eighth Avenue, but most nights I ended up at the dark restless body of water that filled Hempstead Harbor. Lights from Port Washington across the bay glittered in the waves. I leaned on the railing as the wind buffeted my face, not knowing what else to do. It was enough to stand there and feel the cold.

FIRE

Every night, in the rented house with snow falling endlessly, I gathered all the pieces of my life that I wanted to burn. I fed brain tumor information into the fire. A ritual—get the wine, pour a glass, make a fire (I became an expert), and toss in rolled-up magazines and crumpled receipts from Sloan-Kettering. I watched the paper begin to melt, turning black along the edges.

Every night the wind blew. I huddled close in the house with no insulation, in the circle of the fire. I drank wine and fed the fire with my rage, with all that was unacceptable. Every night I collected the pieces and placed them in the kindling pile.

Tony called every night. He became part of my ritual. I was buried in winter's cold merciful arms. I slept, exhausted every night, sinking into the forgetfulness of dreams. I came to sleep like a lover, letting it embrace me and take me away from my shattered world.

See, There He Is

Dear Jeremy,

It snowed again last night. Big fat flakes splattered my windshield. You would have loved it. The road going home around the harbor was ghostly with blowing snow, each light surrounded by a glowing halo. I was alone, slipping past the power plant and up the hill.

We are buried in snow, muffled sounds come from far away and drift over the lawns. It's comforting to be lost in this magic snow world. I don't have to inhabit the real world for a while.

I walked down to the harbor alone and that was perfect, just nature and me—the bushes lost in odd shapes, the warmth of shining lights as I crunched the first footprints into the pure white. I'd rather be outside in wild weather than sit in that house.

Do you miss snow, or me? Probably not your life these past two years. I miss you. Walking seems to be all I want to do, to wander the streets with only the occasional car. I don't even want to shovel snow off the walk. It'll snow again tomorrow.

I shopped last night, found myself at the cookie aisle about to buy Vienna Fingers, but you aren't here to enjoy them, and I don't have much appetite anyway.

All of this feels unreal. What does anything mean anyway? And where are you? Can you see me walking in the snow?

Am I making this up to ease my sorrow?
Love,
Mom

SNAPSHOTS

Jenny at Five

I remember seeing the tall ships when I was five. Daddy and Mommy took us by train. It was my first subway ride. The car rocked and shook and I got scared when the lights went out. When we came to the end, there were so many people I was scared 'cause they crowded around Jeremy and me. I thought they'd step on us, but then Daddy swung me up onto his shoulders, and I saw we were going up a moving stair and turned around to look down. All I could see were people everywhere. Daddy pointed and said, "Look up." I almost fell over looking at the building. It went up, up until my neck hurt. "That's the Twin Towers," he said. We crossed the street to a tall fence. People were climbing it and Mommy held me up and Daddy pulled me over.

It seemed we were at a beach. There was sand everywhere, and those two towers blocked the early morning sun.

I saw tall ships sailing up the Hudson River, one after another, and everybody cheered and screamed, and Jeremy and I played in a big puddle and splashed each other. We got bored, then he and I buried a man in the sand up to his neck. Everyone was laughing.

We stayed all day, lying on the blanket, with only the puddle for water. It was like we were at the beach, but I couldn't find the ocean.

Then I heard music, and Mommy and Daddy stood up and cheered. I heard a boom and the sky exploded. I was scared, but Mommy said, "It's the Fourth of July, remember last year?" And I did, and I was okay. But Jeremy cried and Mommy had to hold him. Big flashes and lights in every color like flowers and more booms until I felt they were shaking my insides and Mommy was crying and Jeremy was holding on to her, and Daddy grabbed me and held me up. I never saw so many people all looking up.

Jenny's Sixth Birthday

I HELD A BLACK AND WHITE PHOTOGRAPH OF MY CHILDREN PERCHED on high stools at the kitchen counter in South Orange, making faces at me. Jenny wore a party hat and rested her chin on her hands. Jeremy grinned. They looked freshly born, sweet and innocent, and I saw the love in their open faces. Seeing the picture, I was reminded of the good times. Sometimes my memory lied, and I believed only the pain and sorrow I wrote about, and not the many more ordinary days of our lives.

I remember Jenny's sixth birthday held in the backyard of our Victorian house; her friends gathered outside, one of them hung by his feet from the tree on the side of the hill. My sister-in-law Lynn set the table while balloons swayed in the breeze.

Jenny at Six

JENNY WAS YANKED FROM HER SUBURBAN LIFE IN SOUTH ORANGE WHEN we left Vinny. No more pink gymnastic leotards or playing with the kids who lived down the hill from us.

As a baby, she noticed any object not in its accustomed place. She pointed, making a sharp insistent sound, which I didn't understand at first. Then I realized: the candles were missing from the mantel, or the chair was moved from the corner. She outgrew this habit when words came, but I saw how observant she was about her surroundings. Change shook her up.

Her world turned upside down and everything shifted. Her father no longer had a place in our home. She coped, yet I saw she was afraid. I pulled my children along on our spontaneous, sometimes chaotic, journey. Maybe adventure wasn't fun, but she had asked to come.

I have a school photo taken the year we left Vinny and moved to Irvington: her sweet young face, her full gorgeous lips, her smattering of freckles, her long tangled hair, her liquid eyes which held an ocean of feeling that her pressed-together lips refused to give voice to.

I was overwhelmed with my responsibilities as a single mother, unable to soothe her or understand what she felt. No excuse. I wish I could reach back to anchor her safely in that changing world.

Jenny at Nine

JENNY AND JEREMY SHARED THE BIG BEDROOM WHEN WE MOVED FROM Irvington, New Jersey, to Queens Village, New York, in 1980. Each had a wall to paint whatever color they wanted. Jenny painted hers pink to match the dotted Swiss curtains on her secondhand canopy bed. Half the bed was crammed with stuffed animals, Bonnie in their midst curled up asleep, snoring. Jenny's friends had drawn on her wall with indelible magic marker. Names, squiggles, and hearts bled through layer upon layer of paint.

On the other side of the room Jeremy's loft bed filled the whole turquoise wall. He slept close to the ceiling. Under the bed, his trains were set up on a green-painted board. Toys were everywhere. So were empty cereal boxes, crumpled paper, and dirty clothes. His sister peered across the divide, disgusted. "He's a slob. I don't want to share a room with him."

Every week I told him to clean up. He didn't listen. After the futility of badgering him, I showed up at his door with a black garbage bag.

"No, no, I'll clean up!" he said, while pushing his favorite Tonka trucks and broken cars into the background.

I grabbed the crumpled paper and empty cereal boxes. "No wonder we have roaches," I said. "Throw your dirty clothes in the hamper and take off those pants. You've had them on for days." This was not my idea of how to spend Saturday.

He threw his toys and Legos into baskets, trailed me as I dragged the junk-filled bag out to the curb.

"Wait, I need that box. No, don't throw that out, I don't care if it's broken"—his litany as he dragged retrieved possessions back towards his room.

Jenny at Fifteen

When we moved to Bayside in 1986, Jenny hated the big impersonal high school where she didn't know anyone. She played hooky for a whole year, no matter how many teachers' signatures to prove attendance she was supposed to get each day. Her teachers responded to me at open school night with "Jennifer Who?"

I came home unexpectedly one day to find her sitting in the living room. I asked why she wasn't at school. She started to cry and told me she hated school. The girls in her class made fun of her. Every morning she walked to school, but when she got there, she couldn't go in. A lot of people used drugs, and she felt pressured.

Now I understood her predicament. I held her in my arms and told her we'd figure it out. After frustrated attempts to find a solution at her school, I vented my anger to her guidance counselor, who suggested a small alternative high school in Manhattan called City as School, which gave students personal attention. Jenny and I visited the next day and met her teachers. Jenny smiled at me. A group of students came over to welcome her and show her around. She walked away with them, laughing and talking.

I watched her leave the house early each day, full of energy, for the long commute into Manhattan by bus and train to the school where she was a person, not just a number.

Christmas 1993

Jenny at Twenty-Two

Mom,
There are a lot of things that run through my mind this holiday season. You've been through so much this year, I wish I could take the pain from you just to make it okay. I realize that I can't do that but I can lend my back to lean on, my ear to listen, and my arms to comfort. I can also try to bring you joy and laughter to brighten your days.

You've been such a pillar of comfort and strength for me through this year. You made a difference to me during pain and hurt, by giving your love and attention to me and my pain, and you continue to do so. I feel very comfortable with you; there's nothing I feel I can't come to you with and I don't think many moms or daughters can stake that claim. I pray for you, Mom, a lot, for life to comfort you, protect, and to constantly let the sun shine on you with love and happiness.

I'm so glad to be with you this holiday season; there's no place I'd rather be and no one I'd rather be with. Being with you is what makes me feel like I've come home in a way that a wooden structure will never be able to do. You always say that you wish our childhood had been easier or that we hadn't moved around so much, but home to us was wherever you were. Home is being loved and cared for, where you feel safe and comforted. Where you laugh, cry, yell and tease. It was your company that gave us those things, not a neighborhood, and I hope that you understand how special that is.

I wish in this New Year, Mom, peace, success, happiness, joy, and most importantly, love. There are a lot of people out there that love you and I happen to be at the head of that line. You're my hero, Mom, and there's nothing I wouldn't do for you.

Thank you for the life you've given Jeremy and me. Every second of it was special and if I were to leave tomorrow, I wouldn't go wanting. I've had everything I've always needed and so did Jeremy. His peacefulness is a huge reflection on your capacity to love and nurture those who you love. We both love you very much. Jeremy will protect and watch you from his special place. I feel that strongly in my heart. I will grow with you, my kids will grow with you, and Jeremy will enjoy every second with us. They say love has no bounds. I believe that the love children who have been cared for have for their parents is incredibly strong. My love and Jeremy's love will always be there with you. Mom, you're very loved and very highly thought of. May this New Year erase the feelings that 1993 brought. Peace Mom. Merry Christmas.

Love always,
Jennifer

Sea Cliff—1994

HOWL

5 February 1994 (journal)

> *Went house hunting today, very difficult. I feel pushed out of my Sea Cliff home. It's been my safe haven. What will become of me? It's hard to think about leaving Jeremy behind. Cast out. Cast adrift. Where will I go? I am lost with no direction, except inward, into the tears and anguish. My heart is broken. It lies bleeding inside of me. I scream and wail and it seems to have no end.*

I sat in Jeremy's room. His not being there was all I could feel. His goneness. The silence. The space where he was not was a vacuum, a penetrating coldness. I held his baseball jacket and buried my nose in its scent of Jeremy, breathing deep.

I woke sobbing one morning from a dream where Jeremy, bone thin, screamed for help, alone in a hospital ward. I heard a voice in my head, *This is how it could've been but wasn't because of all the love.* In another dream I held him as we walked down a hill, trying to get him help. He could hardly stand. I woke up. *No, he's dead.*

I walked around his room, stared up at the skylight. Did he look at the stars every night? When we moved from Bayside to Sea Cliff, I told him to pack up his room. He didn't do anything. He didn't want to move and expressed it by not packing. It was the Fourth of July and outside, fireworks exploded. It sounded like we were being bombed. I told him I couldn't help him. I had the rest of the house to deal with. Whatever wasn't packed when the movers came would be left.

24 February 1994 (journal)

> *I can't believe I can feel this much pain and still be alive. I'm angry because of the struggle to raise my children alone, to work, to deal with all the stress, and this is the outcome? I feel ripped off and an-*

gry that my life has been so tough. Angry he's gone and abandoned me after all I did for him.

One of the big milestones of my first year was Jeremy's birthday on March 9. Jenny and I spent the evening at her home. We didn't talk much about him. I wanted to honor him in some way, but it didn't happen. We were both too raw and exhausted to do anything.

11 March 1994 (journal)
He's really dead. It was his birthday, and he didn't show up. I felt so empty inside. Stunned. Then the day after his birthday, the delayed rush of tears came: intense, furious, shattering. I couldn't stop. I've lost him and he's not coming back. This feels like a truth that has escaped me until now. Or his birthday makes it more real and permanent. Memories of his childhood, his presence, his dying and death fill me endlessly. I feel tormented. I'm in physical pain all of the time.

She goes to work and talks like a normal person, but behind her eyes, if you look close, lives a wild woman who has thrown away nice and pleasant and doesn't want to come down from the roof. She doesn't want to listen to reason. She's outside where it's cold and the wind howls and she's not coming in because she's got a fire in her belly and a dead child in her arms and no one can fix it for her.

Beneath her rage is pain, but she can't go there. The pain will kill her. She's running from it, chucking wood into the fire, wild-eyed and howling, drinking glass after glass of blood red wine.

No one can help her.

The snow had finally melted from the many snowfalls we had that first winter and I drove to Gate of Heaven Cemetery with spring flowers for Jeremy's grave. Right before the gates, I passed the nursery, already festooned with grave blankets and white lily crosses. Once through the gates I looked for the three tall pines that grew at the foot of his grave. Snow piles ringed the parking area and the ground was wet with melting snow.

Vinny's parents owned the plot. Their daughter Suzie had been buried there after her death from leukemia in the 1950s. Jeremy's was the second burial.

It was silent, only the trees swayed in the breeze. I slipped down the muddy hill to his grave—hard to see the dirt covering my son. What I wasn't prepared for was the deep gash that split the earth open.

The ground was bare; no grass or bushes softened the shock. I thought of how chocolate pudding splits open as it cools. I loved to eat the skin off the top, picking it up on a spoon and draping it into my mouth.

I knelt down on the cold earth. I hadn't been there all winter because of the snow. Maybe I needed to pretend it hadn't happened. Now I knew it was true. He had died. I smoothed the earth, covering up the jagged hole that ran half the length of his grave. What I really wanted to do was dig my son's body up and I was horrified. I breathed the smell of wet earth and smoothed the dirt until the crack disappeared.

BOXED

Vinny arrived at my house the following Saturday. He waved a large bottle of red wine as I opened the door. "Thought this would make it easier."

I motioned him in. He walked carefully as if something inside might break. In the kitchen I took the bottle from him, opened it, and poured us each a generous glass.

We attempted small talk but neither of us had much energy for it.

"Well, let's go do it," he said.

We climbed the narrow wooden stairs, lit by the bare overhead bulb, and entered Jeremy's shadowy bedroom. The first room was filled with boxes. On the other side of the divider wall, bathed in sunlight coming from the skylight, were his bed and TV.

"I've already pulled out his games and toys. He wanted T.C. to have his bicycle. I know he's too young for it yet."

"He'd love it."

He sat on the beige carpet by Jeremy's desk and picked up a game.

"I'm so glad you're here," I said, grabbing Jeremy's Slinky off the desk, pouring it back and forth from one palm to the other as I watched Vinny sort through the boxes.

Slowly, the pile grew. We didn't talk much. I discarded word after word. None of them made any sense. I poured more wine.

We didn't laugh much, only once when Vinny picked up Jeremy's green Gumby twisted into a 'Fuck you' gesture. "What's this?" he said, shaking his head.

I said, "I'm keeping that."

I asked how he felt. He shrugged. I said, "I know."

Vinny noticed Jeremy's Atari and video games, "Can I take those?"

"No," I said, even though I would never use them or the Legos on his bed in the other room. I had given Vinny so many of Jeremy's things and had reached my limit.

After we were done, we carried the boxes out to his van. He dropped the back seat and stacked bags filled with Jeremy's life while I wheeled his bike out from the basement.

Sea Cliff—1994

DRUM

THE WINTER BEFORE JEREMY DIED, TONY BROUGHT ME TO A FULL-moon celebration near the Shoreham, Long Island, nuclear power plant. We walked through the woods as bluish moonlight glinted off the frozen snow and arrived at a group huddled around a roaring fire. People talked low and sang songs. After a while, two men sauntered down the hill. They stood in front of the campfire and announced their presence by playing their *djembes*, African drums that were slung in front of them. Electricity shot through my body. Dancing to their rhythms, I felt joyful and full of energy. They told us of a monthly jam held in a church auditorium in Huntington where fifty or more people drummed together.

The beat of the drum reminded me of the rock and roll music I grew up with and the dances I attended every Friday night as a teenager, seeking release, letting my body speak what I had no other means to express.

On that cold January night, the drum spoke and my body answered. That's all I knew as I rose from the frozen ground.

The winter after Jeremy's death I went to the drum jam, led by the remembrance of how the drummers had jolted me awake. As I walked through the parking lot, I felt a vibration that grew stronger as I approached the church—deep thumps as if I was about to enter a beating heart. Inside the building my whole body vibrated with the sound of a hundred drums beating together.

Soon I was dancing to the music, leaping into the air, free of any thoughts, feeling my legs move, my arms reaching up, as I twirled through space, howling. I was in a roomful of people, not alone anymore.

I danced until they turned the lights up and people began to leave. My senses were alive. My body tingled. I was surprised by how much energy flowed through me. My ride home hardly resembled my ride there, when I had struggled to even get off the couch. On the way home, I drove with the windows open and the cold winter air filled my lungs. I was joyfully awake at two in the morning. *How was that possible?* I didn't know, but planned to come back.

At the next jam, the leader announced an African drum-making workshop in March. I signed up.

I drove to the workshop, crying. Spring had arrived after the long cold winter. I wasn't ready for it. I was excited by this new adventure, but Jeremy was dead.

I spent twelve hours with a group of strangers making a *djembe*, oiling the wood, stretching the goat skin over the metal hoops and weaving the stiff cord back and forth. Two people held the drum while I braced my bare feet against it and leaned back with all my weight. I tightened the skin until it reverberated with a light touch, and decorated it with green and red macaw feathers. Then I hit the white goatskin with my open palm and heard the deep boom of its voice—my talking drum.

WANDER

The May after Jeremy died, I moved from Littleworth Lane to Cromwell Place. I couldn't sleep the night before the movers arrived, so I wandered the dark house. I stepped onto the porch, which was aglow with the cool blue of the almost-full moon. Many late nights I had walked among the rustling trees with the wind coming off Long Island Sound, stepping away from my life and all its stress. Now I played my drum to ground myself as my world shifted.

The beautiful cherry tree no longer leaned its low limb over the porch steps, shielding us from the world. Jerry, my new landlord, cut it off three months ago after he bought the house and that action severed me from my time there. It was no longer mine; I was a short timer. Maybe having to move six months after Jeremy's death was wise. I was pushed forward into life when I wanted to hang back and hunker down. *What if Jeremy came back and I had moved? Would he know where to find me?*

We had spent so much time on this lovely porch, rocking and talking, or just sitting in silence. I walked around the side porch to the driveway where Jeremy's black Dodge Charger sat. Jenny would take it tomorrow.

The first time I saw this house, I couldn't believe how lucky I was to find such a haven. Now I wanted to leave as much as I wanted to stay.

I went back into the living room and sat on the fireplace hearth where I'd spent the last six months burning brain tumor information, drinking wine as the snow whirled and blanketed everything.

Puja had already moved to a new house a few blocks away.

The sacred space we rested in during the last two years was dismantled.

I climbed the stairs to Jeremy's attic bedroom. What a meager pile to represent his life! I was leaving his bed frame; Jerry said he would remove it when he started to renovate. Its drawers were empty down to the last paper clip; no scrap of his life remained. When we moved in, I had hired two men to take out the window and haul his bed frame up two floors because the attic stairs were too narrow. Now I had no energy for such heroics, didn't even know if I had enough energy to move or envision a life beyond this moment.

I needed to keep vigil that night, as I'd kept vigil so many nights. Witnessing.

DIG

I MOVED A FEW BLOCKS AWAY TO A TWO-FAMILY HOUSE ON CROMWELL Place, which Jerry also owned. I was unable to think, except that I needed a garden. Even though I had a fever, I stood in the rain and brought the pickaxe down, digging into the wet earth. My connection to family had been ripped up. I needed to get my roots back into the ground before they, and maybe I, died.

Each blow splattered mud on my legs. The rhythm of each thud, the sound of falling rain, and my heavy breathing were all I could hear. I dug with no plan in mind except to plant seeds in the ground and watch them grow. I thought of small leaves breaking through the earth into sunlight. I thought of plants nourished to maturity giving nourishment back. I thought of my son whom I had nurtured with my body.

With the next blow, I heard a clink as my axe hit something hard and stopped. *What was in there?* I recoiled back and dropped the axe. I knelt down to look, as the rain dripped off my nose and along the back of my neck. I wasn't sure I wanted to uncover whatever was buried in my backyard.

I hesitated, then thrusting my hands into the earth, grabbed mud and threw it aside. Using the axe for leverage, I pried under the object and dragged it into the light. I saw a glint of gold and wiped away mud and stones. I held a statue of the Blessed Mother cradling her son Jesus. She looked down at him; her veil was edged in gold.

I sat back on my heels and stared. Mud and rain dripped off my cold hands, yet I couldn't move. The house and trees were misty behind curtains of rain. The only thing solid was the statue I grasped; the only sound the dripping water.

My father ate breakfast early on workdays, by 5:30 I think. The night before, he put out the orange juice and all he was going to eat—such a solitary breakfast.

He rose before dawn when he was a kid to milk cows at the orphanage where he lived. What was his life like at Lincolndale? Did he become used to it? The nuns and priests in charge whispered poisoned words, filling the air with noxious thoughts, accusing him of being a sinner. Criticizing him. He treated us the same way. I was angry; later I understood.

I thought of my father in his tender open-heartedness—being left at an orphanage was a huge betrayal. His anger would arise and who to turn it on but himself? He must have done something wrong to be here. Were there any voices that spoke truth or comforted?

Did my mother feel like his savior or his mother, placed on a pedestal never to be taken down? And she, molded by my father's need, was that what made her resentful? I felt her unspoken conclusion that life was drudgery. I pushed her away, refusing to be like her. She probably wanted something different, but she had promised until death do us part. My father pushed us aside so he could get the most nurturing because he had been starved as a child. He didn't allow us to be needy and demanding children. He was the one allowed that.

My father's lonely breakfast—that's my perception. He might have loved the quiet, all of us asleep, the day not yet begun. He could remember being present with nature all those years ago, the light not yet up in the east, the birds only just stirring, the cows mooing as he carried a pail to the barn. Did he have favorite cows, did he talk softly to them? How he loved routine and quiet. How he hated noise or too many people.

I remember the small well-tended Italian gardens in the Bronx neighborhood where we lived, off Gun Hill Road and White Plains Avenue, past the El. Each garden flourished, abundant with tomatoes, peppers, and eggplant. They tumbled over the small hills and ridges right next to the road—a comfort to see. There in the Bronx, I learned nature was a friend I could always go to. The birds flew in from magical places, free to perch on TV antennas and then fly away. Like I dreamed.

Sea Cliff—1994

BLACK

I didn't attend my friend Esther's wedding in Florida, which took place shortly after I moved to Cromwell Place. I had no desire to celebrate or be far from my safe haven in Sea Cliff. At first she didn't understand: I had to come.

> *Don't you remember how you were when David died? I couldn't count on you for anything. Now I'm in the same place. I know you want me there, but I can't pull it off. I can't share in your happiness right now. I don't want to fly or talk with your relatives who will ask me about Jeremy. I want to wear black.*

I had always been reliable, but not now. I was angry with her for not understanding. I had no desire to see Florida, no desire to endure her family's sympathy, their questions.

Esther called Ed her diamond in the rough. She was a feminist yet wanted a man to take care of her—which she'd learned in her Jewish family. This was her fourth marriage, Ed's second. He left his wife for Esther. He was a former Marine, solid and practical.

When I heard about him, I thought, *This will never work*. However, the day I met him, he arrived at my house before Esther. I hugged him and invited him to my front porch. He was a tall man with kind eyes and a big jaw. His gentle conversation put me at ease while we waited for Esther. I liked him. To my surprise I felt he was perfect for her. You just never know what makes two people click into place like puzzle pieces.

She arrived, her eyes flashing with laughter, a rare occurrence since her son, David, had died three years before. She handed me hope along with hugs and kisses. I took a picture of them: she sat on his lap with her arm around his neck. Their cheeks touched. They looked as if they had finally landed somewhere they wanted to be.

I'd known Esther for fifteen years while she lived alone, struggling with money and her son's addiction. Ed too had lost a son four years ago. He'd blown his brains out in his room. Ed cleaned up with a pail of water and a sponge. Esther had been Ed's addiction counselor at the time. He was newly sober, and she had helped him through.

When her son died from a drug overdose, Ed came to his next session and said it was her time to talk; he'd listen. And he did, week after week, ending each session by thrusting a wad of money into her hand. Sometimes he gave her three or four hundred dollars. He refused to hear her protests, just kept her afloat.

She was too distraught to do anything but lie in bed eating Häagen-Dazs ice cream and hugging David's dog, which she had brought home after she discovered David's body.

She deserved every piece of joy coming to her now. A floodgate had finally opened and all the good held in escrow floated her to a new life. She told me she was waiting for the other shoe to drop and shatter her happiness. I told her God had some explaining as to why it took so long to deliver the goods.

Right now I was where she and Ed had been a few years before, having just joined the club none of us wanted to belong to: parents whose children had died first.

ALL THIS TALK ABOUT MONEY MADE ME THINK ABOUT MY PARENTS SITting at the Formica table in our tiny kitchen in the Bronx where I grew up. My father removed the bottom of the refrigerator panel, where the motor was. They hid their cash behind the insulation. Frozen assets. They sorted through envelopes, which they labeled "rent," "car payment," "doctor," "gifts," "movies," etc. They laid out their cash and divvied it up. Although they never taught me, I must have learned by osmosis because years later as a single parent, I was able to stretch six hundred dollars a month to cover rent, heat, food, and gas. When I found work, my goal was to save a thousand dollars, enough to keep a roof over our heads for three months in case I lost my job. During that time, we never ate out or spent money until I met my goal.

I remember calling Esther one day from Macy's. I held a beautiful red silk blouse, but I couldn't get past the frugal voice in my head, *"Ninety dollars?"* I listened to Esther's words, "You deserve it. You work hard for your children. Buy it." I did, affirming the part of myself that desired beautiful things.

After Jeremy died, I had a conversation with God. "I need work but have no energy to make it happen so you figure it out." I must have had God's ear because from then on, money has flowed as I need it.

As a teenager, my parents' money habits eluded me. I spent every penny of my allowance on 45 rpm rock-and-roll records, going each week to the record store, powered by the few dollars in my pocket. My parents urged me to save. I ignored them, preferring to play music on the stereo and dance. I played favorite songs over and over, sometimes fifteen times until my father yelled, "Enough! Turn that off!" Then I'd take my radio and walk the streets with Dion or the Supremes.

THE APRIL AFTER JEREMY'S DEATH, AS A RESULT OF AN INTERVIEW I'd had the previous month, I began working for my friend's neighbor, who owned a design firm. Again I said goodbye to Oscar but told him I would work evenings if he needed help. My boss was a slim woman with long bleached blond hair. She could work a room like no one else I'd ever met. She wore short skirts and high heels, looking the height of New York style.

It was spring, getting warmer, which seemed like an affront—how could life continue when Jeremy's hadn't? After almost six months, dates were adding up—Christmas, his birthday, Easter.

One morning my boss called me over to her desk and told me she was pleased with my work. I think she wanted to know if I was interested in staying on permanently. The office had two glass walls and warm sunlight shone on us. I stared past her to the street traffic on University Place. She asked what my plans for the future were. My reply: *To make it to lunch.*

ALONE

When Maureen invited me over, I watched Jeremy's best friend, Sean, alive and a college freshman. She asked me to stay the night, but I shook my head. I knew she meant well, yet seeing her healthy kids heightened my loss.

There was no reason to go home except I needed to be alone. I couldn't join in their life for long before I envied it and started asking myself, *Why him? Why us?* When it became too hard, I'd get up to leave.

I didn't know where I belonged, but I didn't belong there.

Maureen listened but I felt she didn't really understand. How could she, with her two kids staring back at her? Her sympathy made me uncomfortable. At least I could tell my therapy group to go fuck themselves for their normal lives, at least that felt truthful. They listened without trying to make me feel better.

No, I didn't fit in anywhere. So it was best to go home.

At this point, only the dark places seemed real.

I worked at being grateful for little things. As I popped sweet red raspberries into my mouth, I felt them dissolve, leaving the little pits between my teeth. I left the cream in the bottom of the bowl and drank it by spoonfuls to make it last longer.

I brought home a bunch of daffodils, arranging them one by one in the blue vase, so every time I entered the kitchen, their golden yellow reminded me to be grateful.

It didn't come naturally at the time. I needed something for my senses to grasp, to remind me of life's beauty. Maybe one day I would see beauty in death, but that didn't make much sense then. I stuck with the raspberries, or the candle, or walking on the beach at night, training myself to believe in the world again.

Sea Cliff—1994

SWEAT

Shortly after Jeremy's first anniversary I received a healing from Puja. I had survived a whole year and, although still grieving, I knew the only reason compelling enough to live for was spiritual growth.

The following week I met Archie Fire Lame Deer, a Lakota medicine man, and his coordinator, who took me aside and asked if I wanted to coordinate Archie's visits when he came to Long Island. Since Tony had done many sweat lodges, she suggested we partner to bring a balance of male and female energy. Most of the participants knew the rituals, but I had no prior experience.

I was intrigued by this invitation that came "out of the blue." Tony and I agreed to accept the proposal. His major concern was that he lived in Sound Beach, fifty miles east on the North Shore of Long Island, a long way from Sea Cliff.

All my life I had longed for a deeper connection to spirit. No amount of food, possessions, entertainment, or distraction satisfied that longing inside me. The first time I crawled into the womb of the sweat lodge on my hands and knees, sat sweating and weeping, stripped of all pretense and all the outer trappings of my life outside that clearing in the pine forest, I knew I had found what was missing.

An *inipi*, a sweat lodge, consists of a circle of supple willow saplings anchored into the ground, then bent over and tied to form a domed structure. The lodge frame is covered with blankets and tarps until the inside is pitch black. An outside fire pit leads to a pit in the center of the lodge, where hot stones are deposited during the ceremony. After the stones are brought in, the medicine person closes the flap. There are usually four rounds to a sweat lodge and the flap is raised and lowered between each one. In a Lakota lodge, women and men sweat separately.

Three weeks after becoming coordinators, I entered the lodge with the women. The firekeeper brought in glowing stones on a pitchfork and piled them in the pit. Archie sprinkled sage on the hot rocks and they burst into flame, filling the air with fragrance. The flap was lowered and we sat in complete darkness. I felt the heat wrap around me. Archie prayed in Lakota and we sang. Water ladled from the bucket whooshed as it hit the rocks. The lodge filled with hot steam and my body was enveloped in stinging moisture. I gasped for breath. The more I tried to escape from the heat, the harder it became. Each round of rocks brought in, piled higher and hotter, became a further test of my ability to stay present, to not bolt and run. The heat probed into my chest, prodding, insisting, until with a cry, I folded forward and let the tears tumble out.

Each week my body told me, *Yes, we need to do this.*

By Christmas, Bonnie was dying, but I sensed she would stay until after the holiday. On January 7, 1995, she stopped eating and was very weak. I brought her onto my bed. As I slept, I had a dream in which she and I entered the woods with a group of people. We walked with great purpose. She struggled to keep up and I gathered her into my arms. A great feeling of love passed between us. I understood that she could leave now because her job was over. She had passed me on to the next phase of my life.

The next day, Tony went to a sweat lodge run by a Dinéh (Navaho) medicine man named Melvin at the Welwyn Preserve. I had design work to complete, in addition to grieving Bonnie's death. That evening Tony brought Melvin and a few others over to my house to meet me. I was busy working and didn't want to be interrupted. At one point, Melvin looked at me and said, "There is a place sacred to my people called Canyon de Chelly where you can talk to the spirits of your loved ones who have passed."

I stared at him. *How did he know?*

I walked into the woods with this group. Every week Tony and I ran sweat lodges. People came from all over to participate.

The first lodge with Melvin began late in the day. The fire was hot, and when the flap was lifted to let in more stones, smoke swirled out into the darkness. It had started to snow and the ground was white. Sparks from the fire shot upwards into the dark sky while fat snowflakes fell towards the ground and evaporated in the heat.

Melvin knelt over one of the participants in the lodge, a hot coal between his teeth, blowing smoke on the woman as she sobbed. He was a shadow against the fire, long hair hanging down over his bare torso. Another world, consisting of the Webb Naval Institute, expensive suburban homes, and families eating dinner and watching TV, existed beyond the park and the safety of the trees.

Some of my friends didn't understand why I was compelled to sweat every week. Whereas in the past their opinion might have affected my decision, I learned from Jeremy's death that there are no guarantees in life and I began to follow my heart.

I spent time with people who, although they didn't know Jeremy, sat with me as I wailed. Not once did I hear anyone say, "Stop it," or "Aren't you over that yet?" Each week I took my place in the circle around the fire pit and waited for the heat to probe its hot fingers into my body. Sweat and toxins from two years of extreme stress poured out and ran in streams into the earth. Many times the heat was too much and I pressed my face to the cool earth, grateful for a moment's relief.

As I had also experienced with African drumming and dance, I felt much better after I expressed my sorrow, lighter, as if I could bear this loss. Maybe joy still existed even if only briefly. I wasn't isolated, the arms of the community held me up. I made prayer ties, shoulder to shoulder with the women, passing tobacco and praying. We shared our stories. I felt safe listening to the crackle of the fire, the smells of sage and wood smoke my only perfume.

We took our place in line and circled the lodge, knelt in front of the doorway, bent down and kissed the ground. *Mitakuye oyasin. All my relations,* we spoke; then crawled into the lodge until we came to our place. We sat cross-legged on the earth, waiting for the ceremony to begin. *How quiet.*

There were laughter, jokes, and music too. We shared good food after a full day. Here I met Denise when our friend Joe, an asthmatic, had trouble breathing during a lodge, and we wrapped him in a blanket and drove him to the ER. Underneath the blanket he wore wet shorts and mud caked his body.

"What is your relation to him?" the nurses asked, eyeing us in disbelief.

"He's our brother," we said in unison.

"What's his last name and address?" the nurse asked.

I turned to Joe. "What's your last name?"

He told them between gasps. Did I want to explain? I looked at Denise. She shook her head. For weeks, every time we looked at each other, we burst into howls of laughter as we remembered that night in the ER. We became friends and later that year, traveled together to Rosebud Reservation in South Dakota for the Lakota Sun Dance.

Sea Cliff—1995

HEAL

I HAD TURNED AWAY FROM THE CATHOLIC CHURCH IN MY TWENTIES. So many of the teachings I received in parochial school—such as women's subservient role, the restriction on birth control, or that you had to be Catholic in order to be saved—opposed my own beliefs. I craved my own personal connection to God, yet my life as a single mother was so busy I never made the time. My children were baptized, but I gave them no training in my childhood religion.

I remember sitting in my car shortly after Jeremy's first operation, speaking into the silence: "You've got to help me. I can't do this alone." Maybe God, or Creator, or Spirit always walked by my side, but I had dropped the conversation long ago.

Turning to God when life took a downward spiral was such a cliché. Well, that's what I did. All my life, watching my parents' example, I thought I had to go it alone. Now I was down on my knees.

I heard that the spirit world couldn't reach for us; we had to take the first step. What I learned was that when I asked for help, it came. My faith grew. I began listening to the voice that came to me in the silence, cultivating a relationship with Creator.

As Jeremy lay dying, I got no argument from the priest or Vinny's strongly Catholic family when I spoke about what we could do to help him cross over. No matter what our personal relationships with God were, our hearts were open, beyond words or definitions of faith. We were intent on helping our beloved Jeremy.

I questioned my relationship with God as I faced life alone without Jeremy; it was unfair that he died so young. I had to learn to surrender to God's larger plan, even when I didn't know at the time what it was. I had to learn to stop asking, "Why?"

PUJA GAVE ME A HEALING DAY WITH SHARON TURNER, A CLAIRVOYANT energy healer, while she was in New York. I wasn't able to attend so

Sharon scheduled a telephone reading for early November.

As it turned out, Jeremy died before my appointment. I called Sharon, not sure what to expect. She told me Jeremy was okay and that all the work we had done helped settle him on the other side. Despite my skepticism, I felt comforted by her words. She affirmed that the things I had done were important.

My father, dead for twelve years, came through with his wry self-deprecating humor. He affirmed that he was present during Jeremy's final weeks, which is what we had both felt. Sharon had no way of knowing any of this information.

My father admitted that if I hadn't been strong during childhood, I wouldn't have survived his abuse. He asked my forgiveness. I was deeply moved by his words and some of my family hurt and abandonment began to heal.

Sharon told me that my needs were important and I must put myself first. I must take whatever time I needed to grieve for Jeremy. I was not to let anyone pull me away before I was finished. The skeptic inside whispered that she was being paid to say this, so how true could it be? Yet much of it felt true. The deep part of me that surfaced as I dealt with Jeremy's illness listened, amazed that someone understood.

Finally, Sharon said that the reading was a gift to honor Jeremy. The following week a tape of our session arrived. I listened many times, always hearing something I hadn't heard before.

I did my grief work. About nine months later, I called Sharon and had another reading—as powerful as the first. Again I listened to the tape, letting her words shift me.

In April 1995, I called for a third reading. This time she revealed even more about my secret inner world, especially about my intention to commit suicide while in Carrier Clinic. No one knew about this. She explained that my children had willingly come in to hold a space of love for me when I couldn't, so I could walk through that time of trial and choose to live. I couldn't deny her words. They woke me up.

I wanted to know more.

She was teaching a workshop at Puja's home in New Paltz the next month. Although I didn't have enough money, the following week my Aunt Mary sent me a check for $350—the price of the workshop plus enough for a motel. Aunt Mary said I won money in the lottery. My aunts played their nieces' and nephews' birthdays and mine had won. I called Sharon and signed up.

When the workshop day came, I met Sharon and introduced myself. We smiled and hugged each other.

I learned about energy healing that weekend. I learned to hold my own space and not allow others to drain me. I learned about appropriate ways to set boundaries. We did exercises that brought these teachings out of our heads and down into our bodies. I learned how to feel my own body's energy and amplify it when tired or drained. I didn't know what questions to ask first. I loved her honesty; she was very real and down to earth. She didn't want to be our guru, only teach us to claim our own power. My rebellious side, which after my Catholic childhood followed no one's rules, listened. She told us not to place her on a pedestal because she would fall off, calling herself the most imperfect spiritual teacher we would meet. Her words reassured me I was in the right place.

I signed up for her September workshop, right after my fiftieth birthday.

Sharon's work was sacred. The grieving I had done since Jeremy's death taught me to keep my heart open. I wanted to explore where I was now and the road that had led there. I honored the tender and undefended place that had emerged since Jeremy's illness. I had ignored the quiet voice of my heart while busy raising my children and building a career, but now it proved more of an ally and teacher than I ever imagined. Although I continued my life in the day-to-day world, my real focus and passion became the space that had opened up in my life.

Sharon had much to teach me about ways to cope with everyday situations. Memories of my childhood surfaced. I had often felt energies around me that I didn't understand and that scared me. I'd shut down the parts of myself that weren't acceptable to my family or teachers. Now I was being trained to open up my abilities in a safe environment. Sharon went slowly, giving us plenty of time to master each step.

I longed to connect to Jeremy in the unseen world. Often when one of my fellow clairvoyants read me, he came through. During one reading, I was told:

"A young man is standing by your right side. He came in right away. Do you know who he might be?"

"Yes."

"He says he was very close to you. He's smiling."

"Yes."

"I'm getting the initial 'J'.

"Yes, his name was Jeremy."

"Was he your son?"

"Yes."

"He wants you to know he's all right. He wants you to stop crying." Pause. "He's tall and thin. He's laughing, making jokes. Was he a funny kid?"

"Very funny."

"He says when you're sad and crying, you can't feel him. He loves you very much."

"I love him too."

At the time, these readings comforted me. I had a window into his world, a way to check on him.

SLOWLY, I CAME ALIVE AND LEARNED WHAT I HAD PASSION FOR. I TURNED away from the glitz, distractions, and 24/7 energy of New York City. That seductive world was only an hour from Sea Cliff. What happened in the unseen world—the place at the corner of my eye, the fleeting images and feelings, or the person who appears at just the right time—was compelling and subversive.

Sea Cliff—1995

PIERCE

A picture of Meher Baba's serene and beautiful face hung over Tony's bed. I didn't know who Meher Baba was at the time, but I knew he was Indian, probably a guru. Tony sometimes meditated in front of him. Meher Baba was a friendly father, gentle and accepting, unlike Tony's. I think his father wanted him to be tough, but Tony was a gentle soul. His father had beaten him into believing that he wasn't all right as he was.

Meher Baba said different.

Tony laughed a lot and loved to tease people. Laughter was the other side of tears. He just wanted life to be easy, to cut him a break.

His family laughed at him. His sister asked me what I was doing with him. Tony, who held me on the front steps when we received the news that Jeremy's tumor was growing again. To me, he was a man who had not had enough kindness. I cherished the gentleness in him, however, I couldn't figure out where I stood with him. As he put it, we both played our cards close to the vest, neither of us wanted to reveal our feelings. I disagreed with him. I remember when I told him I felt we were good for each other. He responded that something was missing and that hurt me.

My anger was close to the surface, and it didn't take much to set it off. Tony avoided my anger, waiting it out like a violent thunderstorm, seeing what the damage would be after it had run its course. This didn't make it easy for him to feel safe with me.

Tony's estranged wife made it difficult for him to see his three children, and this was painful for him. We were both on overload from the crises in our lives. Good sex was the glue, that and the power of what we had experienced walking together through Jeremy's last year. But I began to agree with him, something was missing.

If I stayed with Tony, I would have to settle into a life that was comfortable to him but felt constricting to me. For the first time, I had the freedom to explore and grow without family responsibilities. I wanted my own life. That's what it came down to. He and I were headed in different directions. The more independent I became, the more he pushed back at me, flirting with women right in front of me. Did he want to make me jealous or let me know he was desirable? I stormed out, not understanding the behavior that continued week after week.

I accepted that he was either content with where he was, or unable and unwilling to go any further. Either way, we were at an impasse. We stopped seeing each other.

Yet each week we continued to attend sweat lodge ceremonies at the Welwyn Preserve. We entered the lodge and did warrior sweats with Melvin, who was preparing for Sun Dance—a sacred four-day ceremony that took place each August at the Lakota Reservation in South Dakota. He invited seven women to come with him, Denise and me included.

At first I had no desire to go. I was told that the best way to participate was to have no expectations. I couldn't take two weeks off from work, but Melvin suggested we fly. Denise and I traveled to Denver, then to Rapid City, and then made the five-hour drive to Rosebud Reservation.

Gun-carrying Lakotas greeted us at the entrance to Crow Dog's Paradise, which is part of the Reservation. They checked our names off the list and opened the gate. We drove to Melvin's campsite near the Sun Dance grounds, where we were told to quickly make prayer ties because the tree was being brought in. We jumped right in and ran with the others to the road where an eighty-foot tree was carried by a large group of men. They struggled under its weight. An eagle flew overhead, following the tree.

A hole had been dug in the middle of the circular Sun Dance grounds, and we watched as ropes were tied around the tree to guide it into the hole. Before the men hauled it up, we decorated the tree with streamers of every color, prayer ties from the two hundred Sun Dancers and their supporters. The wind flapped them into a dance, snaking up and around the trunk. The tree wavered, tilted, and with much teamwork from the men, came to rest. The eagle circled high above. As we exited the circular wooden bower that surrounded the Sun Dance grounds, the sky filled with thousands of dragonflies, darting and buzzing around us. The sun set as we walked back to camp for the evening meal, the last the participants would eat for four days.

About three thousand people were tucked into the trees and fields. The smell of campfires and the sounds of drumbeats, shouts, and murmured conversation filled the warm dry August air. Still not sure why I was there, I turned and walked into Melvin's camp.

Early the next morning we awoke as drums echoed through the camp. An announcer greeted us and the first day of Sun Dance began. We assembled at the bower and watched the Sun Dancers enter for the first time—two hundred men and women, the youngest around ten and the oldest in his eighties, all races and nationalities.

The men wore eagle feathers in their hair and sage bracelets braided around their wrists and ankles. They held eagle-bone whistles in their mouths, and in unison the eerie high-pitched sound pierced the air as the sun rose behind the mountains. The men, naked to the waist, wore handmade red skirts with embroidered designs and symbols. The women wore wraps that left their arms bare.

The morning was still cool, but I felt the heat from the sun's rays gathering power. As I looked around at the Sun Dancers and heard the low steady drumbeat in the background, I was transported into another time and place—not America in 1995. I participated in an ancient native ceremony. A group of Lakota chiefs presided, wearing full eagle headdresses. Archie Fire Lame Deer was among them. After the dancers circled the tree, they stopped.

The Sun Dancers approached the chiefs, who waited under the tree with a bearskin spread out in front of them. The first man lay down, his chest was pierced by a scalpel blade incision under his muscle and a wooden dowel inserted. Blood poured down and was staunched by clay from the ground.

A rope tied to the tree was attached to the dowel, and after he stood, he leaned back letting the full weight of his body be held by his cut muscle. At first it was hard to watch, but this was only the beginning. A man circled the perimeter, dragging over ten buffalo skulls attached to the dowels in his back. Another man was attached by his back muscles to a hitching post that was taller than he was. After he climbed on a rock to reach it, the rock was kicked out and he swayed in front of us. My stomach did flips.

Melvin motioned for us seven women to enter the Sun Dance grounds. We entered from the east, turned full circle before walking to where he stood. After he was pierced, he walked over to his own smaller tree and hooked himself to it. A dry wind blew across the trampled grass. He started dancing. It was twelve hours since the dancers began their fast, but I had seen Melvin's woman bring him peyote tea and hide it under the arbor in the corner where he could sip it unnoticed.

When all the dancers who were pierced for that morning were in place, the drums began. It was as if we beat inside a great heart. The sun rose higher and hotter in the sky. I thought of the four-year commitment Sun Dancers made, coming each year to offer prayers, gratitude for promises fulfilled and help received. It was four years since Jeremy's diagnosis. For four years my heart had been pierced. I hung from my own tree of suffering. I understood that I was here to break free and claim my own power.

Sun Dance wiped my slate clean. For four days I danced to support those who had made the four-year commitment. We cooked dinners—big pots of beef stew simmered on the camp stove. We drew water from spigots and carried it back to the kitchen tent. We washed dishes and cleaned up. I watched and didn't say much, but much was happening. For the first two days, Denise and I fasted in support of the Sun Dancers. When Melvin found out, he chided us: "You must eat for us. This gives us strength." We grabbed bowls of rich beef stew and wolfed it down. I had never tasted such delicious food.

By day three, I was running on adrenaline. At breaks in the

ceremony, I collapsed on the blanket, sure I couldn't get up one more time. But the drums started and I rose with my friends. I seemed to be pulled along on the vibration. My feet and body moved before my mind caught up and I realized I was dancing again. I was entrained with the power of over three thousand people focused together.

Each evening the seven of us piled into our car and drove to a nearby lake to wash and cool off. Throwing shampoo and bars of soap to each other, we dove and splashed while fish nibbled at our legs. We floated in the lake as the sun set behind the hills, the fragrant smell of sage surrounded us.

At camp we kept the fire going late into the night while natives from tribes all over the Americas visited to share news and stories.

On the third night, the women went to a *yuwipi* ceremony held in the basement of one of the reservation houses. The windows were draped with blankets to block out any light. We leaned against the wall on the clay floor. The medicine man announced that the ceremony had been called to heal our friend Ginny, who was ill with intestinal cancer. A Lakota woman requested healing for her son, who had been in a car accident that same day.

A square was staked out and the medicine man was rolled up in a star-patterned blanket, tied, and placed face down on the floor. Denise and I looked at each other, not sure what to expect. We were told that spirits picked people up or grabbed anything shiny. After the lights were turned off, the second medicine man began to chant and shake his rattle. I felt the air become electric.

Lights flashed around the room, rattles flew everywhere—first close to my left, and then in front. Wings flapped as if birds circled the room—a tornado of movement. The effect of being in the pitch-black dark, not able to see what was happening, disoriented me. I couldn't deny my senses and what I experienced.

When the lights came on, the blanket was unwrapped and the medicine man emerged. First he talked with Ginny, then told the Lakota woman her son would be all right. Then he announced that the spirits had a message for one of the women: It's time to let the relationship go and move on.

On our way back to camp, we passed the sweat lodge fires that burned all night for anyone who needed to purify. Volleys of embers shot up into the starlit sky. I heard Lakota groups chanting in the dark. From different directions I heard hushed murmurs, the wind moving through the pines, and dogs barking. This ceremony had been passed down through generations long dead before my grandparents left Italy and Eastern Europe to sail in steerage towards the promise of America. At the same time, the last band of the Lakotas under Big Foot were rounded up after the Wounded Knee massacre and herded into the Pine Ridge and Rosebud reservations. Their descendants slept together that night.

When the final day's ceremony ended, the announcer asked us to line up outside the arbor. One by one, two hundred Sun Dancers filed past, thanking us for our support, which enabled them to complete their four-day pledge. Some cried, some were stoic, some smiled, some embraced us, but from all I felt gratitude. And I, in turn, was humbled by their courage and endurance and honored to be among them, my emotions raw as I looked each person in the eye and thanked them for their gift.

I had a dream around this time. I met Jeremy in a garage as I was getting into my car. I was surprised to see him standing there, healthy with no scar or gaunt body. "Jeremy, how are you?" I asked. "I'm fine," he said. "I'm in college studying Greek history." He bent down to get into my car and I said, "Be careful of your head." He feigned hitting it and laughed. "That's not where I am now."

If he could move on, so could I.

August 1995

CELEBRATE

I NEEDED TIME TO INTEGRATE MY EXPERIENCE WHEN I RETURNED FROM Sun Dance, so I didn't work. I decided to throw myself a birthday celebration, and invited friends from all parts of my life, including Vinny, Kyle, and their children; Melvin and my sweat lodge friends; Maureen and Jim; Puja; Andrea; Helene; Robbie; and Liz. Even Tony was there, though I didn't invite him.

Jenny came over with Alan to help with the party. Alan worked as a bartender so we had a constant supply of piña coladas. I heard the blender revving in the kitchen while Jenny helped me decorate. I bought yellow sunflowers and Jenny gifted me a beautiful purple hand-blown glass vase. We filled it and every available vase and placed them around the house. She filled paper bags with sand and candles and set them among the plants and flowers in my garden. At sunset, she lit them and the tiny flames danced in the dark. My friends brought food, blankets, and tables, and we had a nighttime picnic in the backyard.

About forty people came. We danced, drummed, and ate birthday cake. I felt Jeremy there too, urging me to enjoy, celebrate, and not go silently into my fifties.

PIG

I WAS TAPING MUSIC TO TAKE TO SOUTH CAROLINA ON MY TRIP WITH Andrea and her two friends after my birthday party, my first real vacation since Jeremy's death. I rummaged in the drawer of my stereo, not sure if any of the tapes were blank. I flipped in the next one, heard a funny sound, like someone spitting, reversed it, and turned up the volume.

It was Jeremy, making funny sounds and then unmistakably, pig noises. It didn't go on for very long. I thought of him with my recorder one day with nothing to do, fooling around. Hearing him, I felt as if he was alive in the room. I played the tape over and over, listening to the intimate sound of his breath.

The pig noises took me back to a game we played with each other, a running joke that we surprised each other with. I had started it one summer years ago when my kids went to Vinny and Kyle's house in San Francisco for five weeks. Jeremy had a group of little plastic pigs he played with. One day, while searching for postcards to send them, I came across one with two pigs on it. They leaned over a fence, laughing. I wrote something on the back, signed it from your friends, Oink and Boink, and sent it off, laughing to myself. I knew he'd get a kick out of it. He did.

Later, when he was sick, he received a bunch of get-well balloons tied to a little pink stuffed pig. He used the pig to express feelings that were too tough for words.

The sound of his breath came from the quiet of the tape, like a rhythm. I rewound it again. It couldn't be more than two minutes of his breathing.

This time two years ago, he was fighting for his life, right before we knew the potent drugs would not shrink the cancer, only kill him. I hit replay. *When did he tape it?* He never showed it to me, or said, "Hey, Mom, listen to this."

I remember coming home from work in Sea Cliff to find that pig head first in the yellow blender that sat on the kitchen counter. Another time, I picked up the lid of a pot on the stove; the pig was inside. Once, I opened the front door and the pig waited for me on the wood floor like a faithful dog, wearing my earrings. I yelled out, "Jeremy, that's very funny," and heard his laugh coming from the kitchen.

Yet as I thought about it, much was being expressed without words. Jeremy was like that. He didn't talk about his feelings unless I prodded him, and then not always. I always knew sooner or later what he was feeling. We had a more subtle way of communicating—an intuitive way that flowed—and even after he died, he returned in dreams, or through events like the statue of the Blessed Mother and Child I'd dug up, with messages of comfort.

The week of my birthday, I traveled to South Carolina for a week at the beach with Andrea, Peggy, and Wendy. I had just met Wendy, who had a time-share at Pawley's Island. Every day we walked the three-mile beach picking up shells, sleeping on the beach, or swimming in the warm surf. At night we drummed and danced or told stories after dinner. None of us wanted to leave the house or the beach. We nixed any thought of driving an hour to Charleston or going out to dinner. Everything we needed was there.

Saturday, August 26, 1995—Pawley's Island, South Carolina (journal)
Monday, I'll be fifty. Incredible. I'm not a young girl anymore. I feel venerable, vulnerable, and partnerless. Good, solid, and holy, and on the brink of something altogether new and different. Sitting on this porch, looking out over a storming ocean—full of energy. I sit here resting, looking back, looking in, looking forward. Sadness for the struggles and losses...most profoundly Jeremy.

Something unknown and wild is surfacing from within me. I like it, I trust it, I invite it in. I will not apologize, minimize, or dishonor my Self anymore. I feel my power as I feel the power of the water and the wind rushing around me. I wouldn't trade being an untested twenty-year-old for this place of love and peace that is my foundation—built and created by me, stone upon stone, hewn by the Life I have lived until now.

On my birthday I walked the beach alone, my thoughts on Jeremy and the empty years in front of me. All day it stormed and now, low in the west, the sun broke through the clouds.

I felt a tap on my left shoulder and heard the words, "Turn around." As I did, I gasped. No one was there, but a rainbow arced over the ocean. I ran back to the house where my friends were cooking me a birthday dinner.

"Come outside!" I yelled. At first they seemed confused, but then they followed me.

"Wow, that's beautiful." Andrea said.

Wendy ran inside for a camera. We took turns snapping each other standing on the deck in front of the rainbow.

"It feels like this is Jeremy's birthday gift to you," said Wendy.

Sea Cliff—1995

EXCAVATE

Despite the fun celebrations in August, Sun Dance shifted my world. That fall in my living room, I was reading the chapter in *The Artist's Way* about finances, answering the questions at the back. All week I had been thinking. All week I wrote down every penny I spent. Money was tight, I wasn't working full time. What was I supposed to do? Every word stabbed me with its demand that I look at where I was—alone in the attic, Jeremy dead two years, scared about money.

I grabbed the book, screamed, and threw it at the attic ceiling. It tumbled back down. I picked it up as if it were a wounded animal. I crouched down and with all my might, flung it up again and again at the high ceiling and the light that hung suspended. I heard it slam and turn over and over until it hit the floor. I screamed until my throat was raw and sweat poured down my face. I threw it against the ceiling until I broke its spine.

I screamed at God, "Fuck you, fuck you. I'm not playing anymore. You better make my life better or I'm leaving. You've taken my son, what more do you want!"

I lay on the floor, kicking and screaming, beating my fists against the floor. I sounded as if I was murdering someone. My breath came in gasps. I stumbled to my feet, shaking all over.

My downstairs neighbor wasn't home that night. I was glad she couldn't hear me.

I lost my balance on the steps and fell all the way down into the kitchen. I grabbed the phone and called Puja. Between sobs I asked to come over.

I arrived at Puja's house in a storm of emotion that broke over me with the violence of a sudden thunderstorm. She opened the door and I tumbled into her room. I usually inhaled some measure of peace from the ritual of sage, calling in the four directions and her words of prayer, but not that night.

This time she didn't even ask me what was the matter. She gently guided me onto the floor mat. I dropped without a word. She arranged me on my side while I sobbed like a child. She lay down behind me and held me close to her body, as I let the long hard years crash out onto her floor. I thought of the exhaustion and stress I felt as Jeremy was dying, of him telling me, "I love you so much." It took me a long time to quiet down. Then she rocked me. I wasn't used to a woman doing this, but my body relaxed into her arms.

I heard our breaths, hers calm and mine ragged. My throat hurt, my stomach too. Her window was open and the quiet was broken by soft rustlings and distant car motors. The night, like an unseen force, listened. Candle shadows flickered on the walls and ceiling, someone upstairs flushed a toilet.

Puja had given me *The Artist's Way*. Every week I excavated my dreams. So many of them felt dead or forgotten. I wanted to move forward but grief held me fast. Every fantasy from my youth about what my life would be stood in the shadows, passing judgment on me, asking why I still struggled to survive at fifty, why I wasn't financially secure like most of my friends. I had taken a different path as a single mother. Was it too late now to come alive? Did I have the energy? Apparently not, they seemed to say as they watched me lie on the ground.

"There's not much that makes sense anymore." I told Puja the week before. "Since I got back from Sun Dance, nothing seems important except my connection to Spirit. I've been through too much. I don't fit anywhere."

Things of the Spirit. Great. How did that play out in New York? I needed work, but my relationship with the city was changing. In Manhattan, everyone passed me in a rush, with purpose. I had returned from a journey I couldn't talk about.

See, There He Is

THAT WINTER MY FRIENDS AND I MADE MASKS OF OUR FACES. I COULD hardly look at mine. It looked like my mother! Frightened, I left it in my studio but couldn't go back the next day. *What was happening? Who was I?* I didn't like what I saw. Finally I went in and stared at my face, lying there vulnerable. My heart opened in compassion for this woman and what she had been through, every line written on her face told the story of the years.

I painted rainbows over her closed eyes, purple spirals on both cheeks, filled her with joy and life. I had to accept the past and create a new future. I hung on, nurturing myself through this rebirth, alone in the womb of my home, being kind and gentle, giving myself what I had needed when I was a child.

Sea Cliff—1995

RISE

THE SUN ROSE SLOWLY, ONE INFINITESIMAL INCH AT A TIME. I stared at the horizon imagining light, imagining the faintest glow, wondering if it was all in my mind. Was I making it up? I turned away and turned back. No, there was a faint light, a slight easing of the dark. Gradually the sun rose.

My healing too was hardly noticed in my daily existence, but edged ever onward.

In my life, there were setbacks—anniversaries, birthdays, seeing a healthy young man who reminded me of Jeremy or a freckle-faced young boy. Then I retreated, mourned as if his death had happened yesterday, my breath taken away with the power of it. But I rose to the present.

I remember attending a jazz concert. I was riveted, listening to the saxophone answer the guitar, so soft, almost a whisper. It pulled me down into my heart. *How could I be here? Because I was at the hospital, taking care of Jeremy.* No one in the theater knew my son had died; I listened like everyone else. But I had a secret—I had come from another world, the world of children who weren't home safe in bed. The guitar understood, the sax blew, *Yes we understand. Yes, yes, let us take you up, rock you. Yes, you are here, he is not.*

Tears ran down my cheeks in the darkened theater.

Like the sun, I climbed past the dark clouds and storms. A deep part of me moved forward. Only when I stepped back from my life did I have a glimpse of the grieving mother and realize I had survived. One day I passed the cash machine near 34th Street where a younger me, mother of a dying child, had sobbed, unable to press the buttons.

I still grieved but now there were small periods of time when it lifted. Maybe later that day it happened again—small holes in the clouds that enclosed me, letting in light. I began to believe I might actually come back to life. How could I have survived though he didn't? I wasn't the old me, I was different. Part of this slow process was getting to know who I had become and to meet the one who had walked through the dark. A phrase from Albert Camus gave me hope: "In the midst of winter, I finally learned that there was in me an invincible summer."

PART III
1996-2011

Sea Cliff—1996

LEAVE

In 1995 Jenny began to talk about leaving New York, going south to a warmer climate. How she hated the cold, even as a child! At first I thought it was just a passing whim. Secretly I hoped she'd forget about it. I didn't want her to leave. I was too raw yet, had lost too much family in the last few years.

She told me she wouldn't move for at least a year. But when the year came to a close, we had the conversation again. We were drinking coffee in my kitchen.

"Mom, I found out that my company wants to fire the Atlanta sales rep. I'm going down to see if I'm interested in replacing him," she said.

She must have seen my look of dismay because she quickly added, "I can't stand being here. I'm constantly reminded of Jeremy. I don't want to leave you, but if I stay here, I'll regret it when I'm older. You know, not doing what I want to."

I took another sip of coffee.

"Listen, this is your life, and you need to live it your own way. I don't want you to stay for me." Inside I was crying. I still had a hard time with all the losses. Yet to hold her here wasn't fair. I'd have to let her go, just like I let Jeremy go.

Worry ran through my heart as the days passed, and she prepared for her trip to Atlanta. *How were we going to remain close if she moved away?* Jenny and I had had a more difficult relationship during her teenage years. *Could I count on her to remain close?*

She wanted to take the Atlanta job, but her boss at the company's New York headquarters hesitated to approve her move. What if she got married and decided to leave? That would leave them in the lurch. When she told me this, my first reaction was impatience with his concerns. I knew he wouldn't ask a man that question.

Jenny liked Atlanta and Alan did too. He decided to apply to the

Atlanta police force. They started making plans, but she was worried her boss wouldn't transfer her.

"Your boss would be a fool to say no," I reassured her. "Look how you turned the New England territory around when you began selling for them. He won't want to lose you."

Alan was accepted as a police rookie with orders to start training in September 1996. Still no response came from her boss. They were going to move in July, even with no final answer. I realized she was leaving while I traveled to Greece for the first three weeks of July. Everything was moving too fast for me.

Finally her boss came around and offered her the job: she would be the company rep for the entire South after she finished the rest of the year in her New York territory.

When she told me, I grinned and told her that I knew he'd come around.

Meanwhile I lost my job at the ad agency. Oscar was no longer my boss and his replacement and I didn't hit it off. I found myself out of work, Jenny about to leave, and in two weeks I was leaving for Greece. My life was in upheaval.

Then I had a most unusual dream. In it, I was packing for Greece and the plane was late. My father and Jeremy were in the dream. My father called the airlines, asking for updates, while Jeremy helped me decide what to take and what to leave behind as I sorted through everything in my house.

When I woke from the dream, I packed for my trip even though it was two weeks away. I pulled my red suitcase to the side of the bedroom, ready to be hefted down the stairs. That same day, a woman called to ask me if I was available to work the week before I left for Greece, with a promise of more work when I returned. One of my co-workers at the ad agency had recommended me. I said yes.

Two days later Jenny visited and asked me a question. "Can I come live with you until the end of the year? I need to finish out the year here so I can get my commission from New England. Otherwise I'll lose all the work I put in. I won't be any trouble and…"

I stopped her right there. "Yes," I yelled, "Yes, yes, of course. I'd love it."

"I don't want to barge into your life."

"Are you kidding? I'd love it. We'll work it out, give each other enough space." I could hardly believe how my life had turned around.

GREECE

I LEFT FOR GREECE TO JOIN A MYTHOLOGY TOUR, FLEW AWAY FROM MY life into an adventure—Athens to Crete, to the beauty of the ancient Minoan culture. In the Heraklion Museum I viewed paintings of men and women, clearly equals, dancing together in joy, leaping like deer over bulls and soaring through the air. I cried for the ease I saw between them, possibilities I hoped for myself.

From Crete we sailed the Aegean Sea to Santorini, the broken cone from an ancient volcanic eruption, and a few days later on to our hotel in Mykonos. After a short boat ride the next day, we landed at Delos, Apollo and Artemis' sacred island, where their mother Leto came to give birth to them in safety. Ancient Greeks considered it their most sacred site; "Delos" means "clearly seen." I was surprised at how barren, desolate, and windswept it was. Not what I expected.

We hiked the mountain at the island's center. The fierce wind whipped my hair into my eyes. I was afraid I would lose my balance so I stopped to tie my hair back and put on Jeremy's baseball cap.

A strong gust of wind snatched it off my head and tossed it down into a hilly field. Jeremy's turquoise blue hat lay upside down in this field of dusty brown thorns, at the mercy of the wind, just like his head lying at the mercy of the surgeon's knife. I couldn't get it back nor could I get him back.

On this barren island in the middle of the wind-whipped Aegean Sea, I was being told something. "Leave Jeremy's hat here. Leave your son. You can't bring him back. You must go on alone."

I opened to the grief again, sitting on the hill, looking out over this unfamiliar land and sea. Finally I climbed to the top. The wind was so powerful I thought it would blow me off the cliff.

How fragile life was!

Take this from me. I cannot hold this anymore.

Norm, another member of the tour, walked by and, through tears, I told him I'd lost my son's hat. I sat for a long time and then climbed down the mountain.

Jeremy's hat was gone! *Had someone come by and taken it? Someone who couldn't know how special it was to me?* I looked everywhere for it. *Had the wind picked it up again?* I wandered the island in a daze.

Later we took the boat from Delos back to Mykonos. Towering waves slammed the boat until we were afraid we would roll over into the sea.

Our group was leaving for home early the next day but my two friends and I were staying in Greece for ten more days. I came downstairs to say goodbye to these people who had become my travel family.

Norm sat there with Jeremy's hat on his head, smiling. I stared and then threw my arms around him. Through sobs, I thanked him.

What was lost had been found. My open heart understood the message howled by the fierce blowing wind, no translation needed.

Sea Cliff—1996

REUNION

IN EARLY SEPTEMBER 1996 AS PROMISED, JENNY CAME TO LIVE WITH ME for the remaining four months of the year. Her boss had agreed to let her finish the year in New York so she could collect the commission she had worked so hard for.

I thought of all the years Jeremy, she, and I had lived together. What a long road the three of us, now only two, had traveled. Jenny's homecoming was a gift—a new beginning. Here we were after three years, three years in which everything had changed, starting with her brother's death.

She looked so vulnerable sleeping on my gray couch. My living room was the largest room in the house, yet her presence filled it. Her legs lay over my lap and I felt their warmth through my hands. I watched her breathe, her mouth slightly open, her expressive hands quiet now. Open like cups. No longer my baby, she had her own life. *Who was she now?*

She felt like a stranger. I wanted to give her what I couldn't when she was seven but it was too late for that. *Was I strong enough to give her what she needed now?*

It was dark outside and we hadn't had dinner. I watched her sleep as I used to when she fell asleep in my lap after nursing, a thin stream of milk tracing its path down her cheek, dripping into the folds of her neck.

Her brother's death was a wedge between us. No, it united us. Maybe that was why we were here, to learn who we were now as a family and to come alive again.

She slept with her arms tossed back, at peace. She wouldn't do that if she didn't feel safe. I rubbed her feet gently, remembering the first time the nurses brought her to me and I counted her toes; now they smelled from her sneakers. She mumbled and turned over.

Who was Jenny, really? Who had grown from our first meeting, when as a newborn, she picked her head up and peered around the room, wondering, it seemed, where she had landed. I loved her curiosity and began to see the tender side she hid during her teenage years while she broke away, leaving home at seventeen. Maybe I hadn't looked deep enough. What surprised both of us was the ease and humor we shared with each other as adults.

Jenny's presence in my home was a great comfort. I wondered if she felt that way too. We drew closer, creating a safe space in which to rest and soothe the wound that hadn't healed yet. We seemed to be on our best behavior, not from fear, but from love.

Most days we drove to the LIRR train station and rode into Manhattan, reading or sleeping in comfortable silence. We said goodbye in Penn Station and I headed to my freelance job as a promotional art director.

A few years before, when I worked in Soho for a graphic design firm, Jenny took the subway from Queens Village after school to shop on Broadway at Canal Jeans or walk around Greenwich Village. She loved the funky art vibe of this part of the city. She came back to my office after work and showed me what cool purchases she'd bought with her babysitting money.

In one of our many talks during those four months, I said to her, "I wish I could find a man who treats me as well as you do."

She nodded her head, "I know what you mean. It feels like we're healing one another."

We became friends, as well as being mother and daughter, and learned from each other's lives without some of the earlier family baggage.

I bought contact lenses for the first time and had trouble taking them out. Late one night, Jenny listened to me struggle for an hour. "Just put your finger in your eye." she yelled.

"No, no. I can't." I sat in the kitchen with a hand mirror. I couldn't sleep with them in. I washed my hands, but my eye snapped shut every time my finger came near.

"Shit!"

Again, "Just do it."

I'd only had them a week. Every day I wondered what I'd do if New York City's dirt flew into my eye. *Could I take them out at work?* Tonight sweat trickled down my back. The more I tried the worse it got.

"Shit!"

Noise upstairs of Jenny getting up. Her feet clumped down the stairs. She was half asleep as she came towards me. "Take them out already, or I'll take them out myself." She advanced, clicking her long red fingernails together like an insane crab until she was in my face. I must have had a look of horror because she burst into laughter and sat down on the bottom step.

I laughed too, and took the lenses out.

JENNY TALKED ABOUT JEREMY AS WE COOKED DINNER, MAKING ENOUGH food so we could bring home-cooked meals to work for lunch.

"I took him to kindergarten while you ran for the bus. That wasn't easy 'cause he kicked and screamed, running after you. Every morning was the same. I promised him candy when we got back or that I'd play a game with him. One time I found him filling his yellow dump truck with pill bugs, crying in the dirt.

"What's wrong?" I asked him.

"Nobody wants to play with me."

"I dumped out those awful bugs, then said, 'Let's play a game.'

"He looked up to me. I was his second Mom. You were gone a lot when we were young. Who else could he confide in?

"When he got sick he told me he was afraid to die. He wanted to go to medical school even though I knew he'd never get there. But I couldn't say that. I went to my room and cried. He entrusted me with all his hopes and dreams. Now I don't have him to share my childhood memories with. Someday when I stand at your grave, I'll be doing it alone."

In four months, we built a new foundation, a new idea of what it meant to be mother and daughter. We intertwined our lives together, but lightly, no demands or expectations. At the threshold of her move to Atlanta, we strengthened our relationship and learned once again that nothing is taken away without something being given back.

How would my life be when Jenny left? At first I tried not to think about it, but as the months went by, I wondered.

I didn't know yet that her move south would plant the seed in my mind for a simpler life, an easier life, which I would be shown in Atlanta. She moved, but didn't leave me behind. She took me forward with her into her new life, and I went willingly.

I DROVE JENNY TO LA GUARDIA AIRPORT A WEEK BEFORE CHRISTMAS. Our four months together were over. I was driving to Atlanta for the first time the following week.

She hugged me and said, "See you soon." We never said goodbye. It sounded too final.

After Jenny left, I understood what it felt like to be alone. I had friends and had started seeing Tony again, but the sense of family had disappeared. When my mother moved to Colorado to be near my brother and his family, I was left behind. Now everyone had gone on except me.

Why was I still in New York? Family was running out of my clenched hands like sand.

Atlanta, Georgia—1997

SEED

The following spring I had a window seat on my first flight into Atlanta. As we started to descend, I watched the landscape below evolve from scattered houses to small developments until we crossed a major highway, and the skyscrapers rose in the distance. The earth, where small farms broke it, was red—good Georgia clay. I was still getting used to my daughter living in the South, though the plane ride only took two hours.

Jenny waited for me at the airport. We hugged quickly and I heaved my suitcase into the back of her Jeep. I was surprised to see trees with green leaves at the end of March. We were locked into late winter up north.

Rameses, Jenny's black Rottweiler, ran to us as we opened the door, wagging his back end and the stump where his tail should be. He leaned against me as I reached down to hug him, our usual greeting.

Jenny made a pot of coffee and we settled on her deck to catch up. I didn't care what we did all week. I was here to spend time with her, like we had in the past, time to hang out and talk, watch the *X-Files*, and cook food together. Since her work was still slow, she suggested we drive to Chattanooga.

Pots of petunias and pansies already bloomed, and I shed my jacket, letting the warm sun soak into my winter-weary body. I leaned back and sighed. When I drove down at Christmas after she first moved, I didn't needed a winter coat then either. Now the air smelled like spring, a preview of what New York would be like in six weeks.

I have forgotten much of what we did but not the feeling of being in Atlanta that first spring—how the warmth soothed me, like I'd swallowed the sun and my insides were radiating a joy that made me laugh. There were other lives out there, other places to live.

I had expectations of what I wanted from my visit to Jenny, but this wasn't one of them. Surely New York City was the center of my world. But Jenny thrived in her new home, in a new setting, and that realization planted a seed of possibility in my mind, a thought that grew over the next year.

Our visit remains a kaleidoscope of images flung up from my memories, typical of what we did together. I remember Alan coming home from work in his uniform, taking off his gun and the bulletproof vest he wore. For the first time, I understood how dangerous his job as a police officer was.

On Saturday we ate at an outdoor restaurant. I looked around at the tables filled with people having a good time and felt released from some preconceived notion of how I expected life to be. It could be like this.

Sea Cliff—1997

BURNT

Tony and I had been together again for a year when we planned a vacation in September 1997 to the North Fork of Long Island.

Our time together was strained. I had a big web design job going on in my absence and every day I called my team from a local pay phone to keep the work flowing. I realized I had already decided to leave Tony; our vacation was a weeklong goodbye. We weren't growing as a couple, and I had no energy left for trying. We kept coming back to each other and then leaving. Neither of us could figure out what wasn't working.

We drove back to Tony's place, bringing leftover food from vacation. I helped him unload his suitcase and shopping bags, then was ready to leave. He picked up the mail lying scattered in the front hallway. I heard the liquid hum of the fish tanks.

"Want to help me eat some of this food?" he asked. I started to shake my head, then said okay. I fell into the familiar ritual—set the table, spoon out vegetables and pasta, and butter the bread. I paced the room and couldn't stop. Late afternoon sun slid in through the curtains.

Tony shoveled corn into his mouth while he read the mail. He sighed, ripped open another bill. The phone rang.

"Hi, Trish." I heard him say as he talked with his friend. I knew it would be a long call.

I gathered my keys, bag, and sweater. He came out of the bedroom with the phone, laughing at something. How he loved to yak on the phone. But he saw I was ready to go. I stared at his black hair, his mustache streaked with grey hair, and listened to his deep voice, soaking it all in for the last time. The dust motes lit up the secondhand furniture.

I waited weeks for him to answer my questions. Like a well, it took a long time to hear the rock hit the bottom. Nothing changed. I'd hoped it would be different. When I slept here, my dreams careened around the same sickening track and I woke exhausted. We had been through so much together. Maybe. Maybe…

No. Not this time. I knew that was the trap. I turned to him. He held onto the phone conversation like a lifeline as I kissed his cheek and went down the stairs to my car. He stood in the doorway, his face ashen, and continued to talk. Maybe he thought I'd come back again, but I knew I wouldn't. This was finally goodbye.

I backed out of the driveway. He waved. His image was burnt into my brain: one leg crossed over the other, leaning on the door frame. His face was shocked, like a little boy after his father struck him.

That was the last time I saw Tony, although we still talk by phone. The love we had has not died, but our time together was over.

Ireland, 1998

RELEASE

I KNEW HOW RELATIONSHIPS CHANGED, HOW PEOPLE ONCE CLOSE GREW apart. A family collapsed when the central person died. Dust and memories were all that were left.

As the changes happened, I clung to Jenny, maybe not in typical ways—daily phone calls or demands—but I clung to the desire to hold her close, like in the four months we'd lived together.

Even after she moved to Atlanta I held on, a kind of delayed response to the empty nest. It kept me from feeling alone in the world. Powerful medicine. It worked for a few years, allaying my fear that her move would result in us becoming distant relations...and then what?

I saw another chance to bring us closer when I suggested what she wanted most—to see Ireland where her father's ancestors had lived. We were still navigating turbulent waters. Could we hold together? Were the ties of love strong enough? As she struggled with the great loss of her younger brother, she needed to find her own way in life without the burden of also filling the hole inside me.

None of this was spoken or even understood during our trip. It took me years to make sense of what made our Ireland trip such a powerful experience.

AT THE DUBLIN AIRPORT I LISTENED TO THE LILTING SOUNDS OF IRISH passengers holding their plump red-faced babies, home for Christmas. They raced into the outstretched arms of waiting family while I ran the gauntlet of eager faces and screams of delight. I found a table and hid behind the menu to cover how vulnerable I felt. Breakfast would help ground me, coffee would set my thoughts right. As I ate my eggs and watched the clock, I envisioned Jenny's plane coming towards me as it skirted the Irish coast and banked into Dublin. I imagined how we would greet each other with delight. I thought of our California trip the year before—the spa, the massages, the room service, wrapped in big fluffy bathrobes, resting and laughing or going to the San Diego Zoo and Tijuana.

She stepped through the airport gate. I walked over to hug her but she pushed past me mumbling, "I need a cigarette." I watched her retreat through the automatic door and out into the early morning Irish air.

Now I imagine her thoughts:

"Don't you know I'm here with my grief? Don't you know I've got a lot on my mind? Don't need me. I'm too full and can't hold anything else. I've brought a planeload of regrets, of never going to be's, of nights curled up under the covers with the phone off. I've flown into the rising sun, into another world and he's not here either."

She stubbed out her cigarette, sighed, and returned to me.

IRELAND HAS A DEEP SOUL THAT I FELT ESPECIALLY IN THE COUNTRYside's stone fences and crumbling churches, the fierce winds and surf of the west coast, the land green even in December. The sun didn't rise until nearly nine and it grew dark around four but we searched, map in hand, driving on the left side of the road with the driver on the right side of the car. I circled the roundabouts until I figured out how to leave without causing an accident.

Rounding a corner in Ennis, Jeremy's twin walked towards us—same dark hair, same tall thin body. For a moment our minds scrambled, wish became real but wasn't. Could it be? No, it was only an echo. When was the end the end? The longing goes on.

Were we driven by a deeper need we hadn't even articulated? Did we hope to reclaim Jeremy, to find a balm for the hole he left in our lives?

On the way to the Dingle Peninsula, a hay wagon rounded the bend, taking up the whole road. Could we pass each other on such a narrow dirt lane when the sides were high hedges? Somehow we squeezed past, hearts beating.

We walked an early morning sun-bright path at the Lakes of Killarney, deer grazing in grass and moss still lush green. Mist rose from the silent water. We talked as we strolled around the lake. Jenny cut me off in mid-sentence with a frown, pushed on ahead. I watched her back recede, left behind in confusion.

The beauty of the land was breathtaking, green but wild, craggy and raw, as we drove through the rain to the Cliffs of Moher. The sea was somewhere below, lost in a fog that shrouded everything until only shadows emerged and faded away. The man in the gift shop said that although we could hear the sea breathing below us, we wouldn't see the cliffs that day, only rain and mist. Small breaks in the fog enabled us to glimpse the sea sucking against the rocks far below, nothing between here and America but the cold ocean. Mist bathed our faces, softening everything. We wandered uphill towards the faint outline of the viewing tower, wind so strong it blew a small tumbling stream back up the cliff into our faces. Baptism. A faint glow hinted at where the sun shone. I thought of Fatima's miracle, the sun burning through everyone's doubts.

The clouds broke in a slow dance, revealing the hidden cliffs. The coastline emerged like seeing after being blind—an undulating line faded away into the distance, the clouds herded inland by the wind, dissipating in the bright sun.

I'm sensitive to nature's messages: *you are here to wipe the grief from your hearts. What seems unlikely is actually possible. The winds of change are clearing away your vision. A new life awaits you.*

AT A KINSALE INN WE HAD OUR PICK OF ROOMS BECAUSE IT WAS OFF-season. We ate a sumptuous dinner and talked like so many times before. I got the impression she was telling me she needed our relationship to change, saying words I have a hard time remembering. It's as if I had amnesia. Her need for space in which to mourn was healthy, but I misunderstood her words. Five years now since Jeremy died, two years since Jenny left. I could see she was settling into her own life. Was she leaving me behind? If I couldn't hold onto her, where did that leave me? What if she slipped away like Jeremy had? I knew how easily that could happen. But these changes didn't mean Jenny and I would grow apart as I feared. They were just another step in our growth as mother and daughter.

I laid in bed that night in the dark, my whole body on fire. Something hard and necessary was being consumed in flames. I surrendered and let it wash over me. I realized I had to move on and find my own way too, although the voice inside that urged me to leave New York was still only a whisper I barely heard.

I returned to Sea Cliff and lost my freelance job. Two weeks later a woman called from a children's book publisher. Did I want to come work for them? A teacher would soon enter my life to help me develop my writing. A new phase had begun.

Jenny and I left the grief we couldn't carry anymore and let the green soul of Ireland heal us. We had stood on the Cliffs of Moher watching the Aran Islands come into view as the fog rolled away and the sun dried our faces. Across the ocean America waited.

Sea Cliff—1999

BUZZ

In December 1998, shortly after I returned from Ireland, I found myself out of work. I called a woman named Leslie from a children's educational publisher who had called me the previous summer. I had been busy, but now I was available. She asked if I could start the day after New Year's.

When I arrived at their Fifth Avenue office on the first workday of 1999, chaos reigned. Boxes were piled halfway up the walls. People worked in little cubicles with papers scattered on the floor and desks. Bookcases buckled under the weight of rubber-banded manuscripts. Wastebaskets overflowed. Editors scurried down narrow corridors. Light filtered in from high loft windows.

Were they moving in or out? I wondered. Either way, it didn't look good. I could see the strain on Leslie's face. She confirmed that they were in the middle of a move, while at the same time a huge deadline with McGraw-Hill was due. They'd hired production people off the street to finish.

My job was to hire illustrators and sketch out ideas. I shared a back office with four other designers. The only window faced a brick wall across an alley. There was no heat—I worked in my coat. Although I had to call illustrators, there was no phone in the room. I had to walk to the front desk and use their phone. *This doesn't look good*, I thought.

The next day, I watched as my four office mates packed up and left. Their desks were wheeled out. The next day I had no desk; my computer was on the floor. *That's it*, I thought. *What am I doing here?*

After eighteen years in my profession, I felt demoted to the last circle in hell. I slumped into the chair facing the alley and watched huge snowflakes slide past in the gray winter half-light.

After three weeks of working amidst an ever-changing landscape of broken chairs and frazzled art directors, with only the most basic supplies, Leslie called me in. She scowled, telling me that the production manager wanted me at the new offices to design a series of children's guided math readers. She was upset that she was going to lose me because I was doing a great job.

I walked across Union Square feeling free and ready for an adventure. The new offices were quiet, stacked with cardboard boxes being moved daily from the old office. I followed a woman named Jennie back to a corner office where I heard the buzz of activity and laughter. What a welcome change. I entered a big room filled with tables, chairs, props, and boxes of fabric, toys, and jewelry tumbling onto the floor. Jennie introduced me to the group. One man gave me a big hello and others stopped what they were doing to wave.

Before I could ask a question, Jennie handed me a book and asked me to design it. The other six designers sketched toys and set up props. I wasn't sure I remembered how to lighten up and play. It had been so long.

I watched them as I settled into this strange but compelling environment. I was having more fun than I'd imagined, as if I'd been let out of school.

I knew how to organize a team, ask the right questions, and get the job done. I was a good designer. Here I found my work family. Most of the editors, designers, and production people pursued other creative avenues outside work and were fun, competent collaborators. One woman ran a publishing company with her husband, one was an opera singer, and my office mate was a fisherman on the weekends. Of all my jobs, this was the most satisfying, the most challenging, and the one that most deeply engaged my heart. I loved creating beautiful visuals and stories that would touch the hearts of inner-city children with messages of inclusion, acceptance, and encouragement for their unique spirits.

Sea Cliff—2000

SEARCH

I was standing on 14th Street in New York City smelling bus fumes and piss, waiting for a bus to take me to Penn Station when the scene faded, like it was a dream I was waking from. What I saw in front of me was a picture of how I wanted my life to be—living among the trees, close to a river, with a partner, our friends coming to visit—a simpler life.

But that was not where I found myself that day. My dream stepped forward fully formed, as obvious as my name, and I had to find where to plant it.

I had discovered a new and completely different path, and my life as it was ceased to matter in the same way.

EVEN THOUGH I'D LOVED WORKING AT THE CHILDREN'S EDUCATIONAL publisher for the past two years, my life had grown stale. I rode the same LIRR train to Penn Station and, depending on the weather, either walked to Union Square or took the subway.

I walked the same streets in Sea Cliff that I had walked for the past eight years, noticing that the juice I once felt was gone. I thought about Jeremy, Jenny, Tony, my sculpting class, and the sweat lodges—all the people and places I enjoyed so much—all gone from my life. For a while I embraced the ease, after many years of upheaval and stress. Travel to Ireland, Egypt, the Southwest, and Mexico gave me adventures to look forward to, yet each time I flew back to New York, a quiet voice whispered, *It's time to go, you're done here.*

Sea Cliff started to constrain me. Since I couldn't afford to buy a house, what was my future there? The energy that had brought me there had disappeared. In New York I was constantly revisiting my past.

The search for a new home frightened and also excited me. I was about to tear up the roots I put down in the town I loved more than any place I'd ever lived.

My friend Vijay had been calling me from the mountains of Western North Carolina with tempting conversations—it was January and sixty degrees. This as I froze, bundled up in New York. I agreed to visit Asheville.

When I lived with Puja, she introduced me to Vijay, a client of hers, on my front porch in Sea Cliff. He published a Long Island-based spiritual magazine called *Creations*. We shook hands. I felt at ease with him, liked his friendly smile and wild curly hair. At the time I didn't know I'd just met the friend who would lead me to the next stage of my journey.

One day I had a session with Connie, Vijay's partner, an emotional release therapist. I expressed my grief about Tony and the confusing changes in my life. When I left the session, feeling lighter, Vijay asked if I would be interested in designing the next issue of *Creations*. His designer had quit and he was in a bind to meet the deadline. I said yes.

Vijay and I high-fived at the end of the project. It had gone smoothly and I enjoyed working with him. I asked if we could continue our relationship after he moved to Western North Carolina. He too had enjoyed our working relationship and said yes.

COME

In May 2000, on my way down to visit Jenny in Atlanta and Vijay and Connie in Asheville, I decided to take a detour to the Skyline Drive in Virginia to hike. At the information center, the ranger suggested the trail to Doyle's River Falls. The trail was steep, long, and hot. I wondered if I should do this, or if I should turn around and get going. Towards the bottom, the trail leveled out and crossed a small bridge over the river. As I came skidding down, momentum carrying me at my New York pace, I saw the doe.

She strolled down the hill to my right. I stopped short. She didn't run. I would have, if a strange creature came crashing through the woods. She calmly eyed me, then continued grazing. Oh, to have no cares but to eat from the plenty surrounding me!

Jenny commented after my midnight arrival that she had to wait up for me as a result of my hiking in the woods communing with the deer.

I laughed, told her it was my vacation. I liked her new place, an industrial loft with exposed pipes, air conditioning ducts, and brick walls. I knew the move was stressful because her former landladies had pushed her out three weeks ago.

Jenny wanted me to paint her dresser. I wanted to rest, not work. I told her I'd rather paint the alcove in her bedroom as a birthday gift. I created a window with colorful wildflowers, blue sky, sun, and two bees careening in from the right. She loved it and turned her bed around so she could see it when she opened her eyes in the morning.

For three days we hung out in the muggy spring heat of the city. I could tell something was troubling her. Was she still sad over her breakup with Alan?

When it was time to leave for Asheville, I found it hard to say goodbye. So did she. We lingered and talked. I was worried about how stressed she was. I drove away with a cord of love and concern that stretched as I drove further north.

I didn't want to like Asheville.

THE TRIP TOOK LONGER THAN I THOUGHT. DRIVING UNFAMILIAR HIGHways in the dark disoriented me. I chose the first motel in Asheville. It was two o'clock. All I wanted was to lie down and sleep.

Georgia had been sunny and hot. The mountains of North Carolina were drenched with rain. I dropped my suitcase on the motel room floor and crawled into bed, listening to the steady drum of rain outside.

I woke in the dim gray dawn from a dream where I stood on the New Jersey Palisades looking back at New York City in the distance. It was a dream I'd had before. Manhattan was in flames.

I pulled back the curtain, excited about seeing Vijay and Connie again, of exploring this land they loved. I squinted, hoping to see mountains, but mist and rain shrouded the far distance.

By the time I stepped outside later, the rain had stopped and mountains surrounded me.

I called Vijay and waited for a call back. In the meantime, I drove out of Asheville and onto the Blue Ridge Parkway, where I saw signs for the Folk Art Center. I almost wept over the beauty that these artists from the Southern Highland Craft Guild created with their loving hands using natural materials. I felt new possibilities. Here I could finally fan the flame of creativity into a fire.

I finally connected with Vijay and followed him to Black Mountain. Their A-frame house nestled in the trees. Connie greeted me, saying, "Welcome home," showed me to a room that was painted purple. Yes!

For the first time in a long time, I felt grounded and at rest. It was how I felt when I first moved to Sea Cliff. My body, faithful companion, didn't lie.

I slept in the arms of God that night, like I had come home.

I was tired, weary to the bone. The beauty of the land revived me. I didn't always have to push a rock up the hill. From here New York seemed far away and all my connections there less compelling. Could I live in a different way here? I couldn't continue with everything in rigid time frames. Who would I be after six months or a year in Asheville?

Vijay drove me to the Lookout Mountain trailhead the next morning. He said I could take the easy trestle road or the trail to the top. There was no question in my mind. I was going straight up the rocky path.

I climbed to where I had to haul myself up using hanging roots for handholds, and scrambled up rocks I could hardly scale. Even though it was still morning, the sun was hot. Sweat ran into my eyes and trickled down my spine. I could taste the salt on my lips. The last steps were built right into the rocks, and then I was on the outside of a rocky slope on hands and knees. My fear of heights rose, to my right only air and a gorgeous view west—mountain upon mountain fading away into softer shades of blue. I kept going, wiggling through a narrow passage in the rock face.

I stood up, gasping. The top. I turned in a complete circle—a 360-degree view of green mountains. There were no houses or streets visible, only US 40 snaking away into the distance, disappearing into the folds of the Appalachians. A hawk circled below, barely moving his wings in an updraft. A steady wind dried the sweat from my face.

Yes, I was sure. I would leave New York.

ON THE DRIVE BACK TO SEA CLIFF, I REMAINED IN THE MOUNTAIN energy, calmed down, yet wondering how I could move my life south. The closer to New York, the more I wanted to turn around. Images of my life flashed by, each one pushed me further into the raw place I held at bay. All through Pennsylvania I cried. I didn't want to go home because it didn't feel like home anymore. I cried for Jeremy, because I was going on without him. *Was this what it felt like when one died, all those images rolling past like a film strip?*

When I crossed the George Washington Bridge, the intensity of New York assaulted me. I struggled to hold onto the mountain peace. No trees, only tall buildings and red taillights in front of me. Traffic was backed up on the Cross Bronx Expressway. I envisioned a long slow crawl home. Horns honked, cars cut in front of me, pushing for every inch of space. I was back in fight mode. Smoke and exhaust fumes filled my lungs. I closed my windows, so much for fresh air. How had I lived with this level of stress and stimulation for so long?

Traffic stretched far away into the distance. Two hours later, I turned off at the Sea Cliff exit and slowed down at the harbor, letting my breath out. Finally, I screeched to a stop in my driveway, too tired to think of food, the supermarket just another hassle. I was betraying my hometown—I had found a better place.

My heart brought up reason after reason why I should go and why I should stay. Each one needed an answer. I had to get clear.

See, There He Is

I returned to Asheville in August to housesit Vijay and Connie's cats while they vacationed. The memories of hiking to the top of Lookout Mountain and waking in peace brought me back.

I left Sea Cliff, crawling in traffic. New York didn't want to release me. Once I crossed the Hudson River, I sped away. In Virginia I was finally able to take a deep breath. I drove, thinking about my life, about Jeremy, about how my life in Sea Cliff began. Of how I used to feel like a motherless child but didn't anymore. Sea Cliff healed me. I came in from the cold, created a wonderful life out of the ashes and the tears.

With all the rain, the earth felt moist and lush. I longed to bury my face in the emerald green and let it wash away all traces of the old.

I felt peace at other times, in other places, but the Southern Appalachians vibrated with it. All I wanted was to sit and soak it in. Even though I was ready, it wasn't easy to settle. It was like lowering myself into a lake, bit by bit. I kept busy, to push away my fears. How did I make peace with peace?

All the next day I looked at houses with a Realtor, found a few but wasn't ready to make a commitment. I headed back to Vijay's house wondering what I was doing there.

The nights were black-dark. The huge windows made me feel exposed and vulnerable, so I retreated to my cave-like room. The crickets sang loudly, nature outside breathed, humming and alive.

What was with me? I couldn't seem to get enough sleep. I sank into the earth, into myself, exhausted. I seemed to be hiding out, feeling sad or at least needing solitude. Did I run so hard that I didn't even recognize how tired I was until I stopped?

I discovered an ice cream store where I could make my own mix of ingredients with nuts, chocolate, peaches, whatever. Delicious. I decided to eat ice cream every day.

I had two interviews in Asheville, and although work was scarce, if I was willing to hustle, I could find it. Again, I felt weary. Asheville welcomed me but how did I make money to live here? I thought I'd find my dream house and move, but it wasn't going to be that easy. I was thrown back into all the wounded places that I thought were healed.

Instead of retreating to my room that night, I wrapped myself in a blanket and sat on the deck in the vast mountain darkness. I listened to the crickets chant a soothing mantra and watched the moon float up through the huge oak in front of me. I snuggled deeper into the lounge chair and let myself be in this unfamiliar world. I sat for hours, filling up with the night sounds, the distant traffic on US 40, and the soft sound of leaves moving all around me.

In the end, nothing was resolved other than that I loved being there.

Back in Sea Cliff, I wondered if I should stay or go? One night I fell asleep in my comfortable chair with the TV on. I woke sometime after two, watched images without comprehension. Soft music filled the room and rushing water filled the screen. The camera panned back to a wooded stream with ferns moving in the breeze. The sun shone through the trees. These words appeared on the screen over the scene: "Come to Asheville."

I sat up and laughed until I doubled over with glee.

St. John, Virgin Islands —December 2000

LEAP

I'd been to Asheville four times since May 2000. Each time I bought food at the local health food store, I pretended to live there. When I came back to New York, I brought the mountain peace with me. I wanted to go, but wasn't sure I wanted to leave my comfortable life.

Finally, before a trip to St. John's with Jenny, I asked for a sign. Then I boarded the plane.

When I landed in St. Thomas after changing planes in San Juan, my luggage didn't arrive. I hailed a taxi and headed across the island to the St. John's ferry. I was dressed in black, carrying a jacket, a refugee from the cold north among people in colorful tropical outfits. I had to buy a bathing suit, shorts, T-shirt, sandals, and toothbrush. What else did I need? I would not let this ruin my vacation.

Jenny greeted me at the dock in St. John's. She had arrived that morning and already looked cool and comfortable behind the wheel of our rental Jeep. She noticed I didn't have any bags and asked if they'd lost mine too. They had sent hers on a later ferry after they found them.

St. John's consists of a series of steep mountains surrounded by a turquoise sea. Our villa was atop one of the smaller mountains outside town. Jenny took me to every room,i reciting detailed descriptions as if she were a tour guide. I laughed at her deadpan humor. The villa's main feature was a deck that jutted out like the prow of a ship. All the rooms on the main floor opened onto this deck. This was better than we could have imagined.

The coastline curved away to my left with each mountain fading to purple. The sun shone, but a storm's dark shape was coming towards us, erasing the island. Soon the wind rose, the sun disappeared, and the furious rain drenched us, yet we didn't go inside. The warm rain would be over in fifteen minutes.

My luggage was dropped onto the town dock by the last ferry. It seemed like an afterthought. I had already stepped onto the island with only the clothes on my back, empty-handed, eager to move forward.

That night I slept on the deck in a hammock, my ceiling a canopy of stars, the full moon like an eye watching over me. I swayed in the tropical breeze that smelled of gardenias.

Each morning Jenny and I lounged in the open-air room that served as the kitchen, drinking coffee and talking. We took fruit from the refrigerator and looked for the iguana that we'd seen peeking from behind it.

We'd traveled every December for five years, the first being a trip to New Orleans after she moved to Atlanta. This would be our last trip before I took the great leap and walked away from my life in New York.

I walked around the enormous villa, shaking my head in delighted surprise, saying, "If this is the doorway to my new life, I'm ready to walk through."

We both knew something large, larger than the storms, was on the horizon. Jenny wanted me to move, I could feel it, and I did too. I was almost there.

What I remember of our week in St. John's:

—*the gaily-painted houses of magenta, yellow-green, orange, and blue lining the shore as my ferry docked and Jenny waited next to the rental Jeep.*

—*the ever-present wind buffeting our villa, blowing her door open every night and how I needed the safe cocoon of a smaller protected room away from the wind.*

—*the little pool on the deck that I swam laps in every day.*

—*the CD ¡Mo' Vida! we bought and played over and over on the living room stereo until the rhythms ran through my dreams.*

—*driving across mountainous St. John's, around steep curves, through the jungle, until we came to the small shack on the beach where we ate breakfast.*

—*the clear turquoise water, how fake it looked to me, raised where water was brown and opaque.*

—*snorkeling off the beach, as the waves rose above me with a gurgle. A pelican knifed the water, scooping up a beak full of fish. I bobbed to the surface. He floated next to me with water draining out of his prehistoric pouch.*

—*Jenny driving to the other side of Cruz Bay late at night to talk to her new boyfriend because it was the only place she could get cell phone reception.*

Each day we sat on the deck before leaving on our daily adventures. We talked like two women friends who knew each other well. Maybe we had passed through an invisible membrane to get here and this was tangible proof that life could be benevolent. Each experience of the paradise surrounding us chipped away at the certainty that life equaled pain. Jenny had a phrase to counter "no pain, no gain." It was "no pain, no pain." I wasn't sure I believed it, but it amused me.

On the way back home, my plane was delayed in San Juan. I slept in the terminal far into the night before they found a pilot who was well-rested enough to fly us to New York.

I climbed into my Sea Cliff bed as the sun rose. I had just fallen asleep when Helen called from the publishing company with bad news. They fired half their staff while I was gone, but wanted to keep me on. Unfortunately, they could only guarantee me seventy hours a month, not enough to pay my bills.

If I needed to find work, I might as well move to Asheville and find it there. I realized this fulfilling job was what held me to New York. I had my answer as to which path to take.

Two days later, Helen called me into her office to ask if I was interested in working on a new project—a contract to design twenty-five children's books. Helen offered me as many books as I wanted to work on, adding that I should put in as much time as needed to finish them. The deadline was the end of May.

For the first five months of 2001, I worked long hours and saved money. My goal when the project finished was to move to Asheville and either rent or buy a house.

After deciding to move to Asheville, I felt absolved of my past, a huge burden laid down. I'd never had this sense of joy and clarity while making such a huge shift. I just had to finish the project and I'd be free to leave.

STING

It started snowing late one evening the last winter I lived in Sea Cliff. I was prepared; refrigerator filled, wood for the fireplace. I lay in bed with the curtains open and listened to the silence, the purposeful flakes heading for the ground. Snow splattered on the porch roof outside my window and I knew the forecast was right—a blizzard, the biggest one in an already snow-filled winter.

When I woke, the trees, bushes, and cars had lost their shapes as snow piled up. No one was out, the road was unbroken by a tire track. No sound except the steady whoosh of falling snow. We still had power so I flipped on the Weather Channel, twenty-two inches or more expected. I called a friend. She was snowed in too.

All day and night it continued to snow. I began to get cabin fever. The next morning I opened my front door to a three-foot wall of blown snow blocking my exit. I had left the snow shovel in the basement but was determined to go out. I bundled up, every inch except my nose and eyes covered. I used a broom to break through but gave up on the steps and plowed through with snow up past my knees. The wind blew snow sideways. Alone, I walked down the middle of the only plowed street, heading for the park at the cliff's edge.

Pine tree branches drooped with snow, transformed into magical shapes. No planes flew into La Guardia. The world had stopped its routine. From the P oint, I looked at the water of Long Island Sound crashing against the rocks below. The distant cliffs of Port Washington on the other side of Hempstead Harbor loomed faintly in the blown snow.

I had lived here for over eight years now, through hot humid summers, autumns radiant with red and golden trees, and tender springs with new life sprouting everywhere. I came here with Jeremy, but he was gone now. I remained, loving this town that had nurtured me, solitary like the great blue heron that perched in the tree, waiting for food to swim by, doing what she needed to live. I needed to live, to feel snow sting my face. I needed to be out in nature's wildest weather. I braced myself against the split rail fence at the edge of the cliff, took deep breaths of the frigid air, my legs cold in their snow-caked pants—sister to the howling wind.

Asheville—2001

JUMP

THE PROJECT WAS OVER BY MID-MAY. I ALREADY HAD THE CLOSETS packed into boxes. I told Helen I was taking a week off to return to Asheville. Jenny was meeting me on Saturday and staying for the weekend. Robbie was visiting the following weekend on her way to see her father in Florida. I even had plans to join Vijay and Connie and their friends at Lake Logan, where they were having a volleyball game the day I arrived.

Should I rent or buy a house? One friend said, "If you buy, you're committing yourself. It's not easy to back out if times get rough."

I found my way to Lake Logan, which was cool and serene after my long hot drive. The volleyball game had started. They motioned me to a side and I started playing. I smiled to myself; this was more fun than I had at home.

Jenny showed up towards evening and we found a hotel for the weekend. The apartment that held the most promise was rented and the next one was located in a small enclave with tall trees on hillsides, flowers blooming on porches. The apartment door was open, the floor ankle-deep in trash, broken furniture, bottles, and old food. Jenny commented that buying any house would be better than what we'd seen.

I picked up a real estate magazine and circled interesting houses. The first Realtor agreed to meet later that day. I told him I was in Asheville to buy a house that week—a statement I'm sure any Realtor would love to hear.

I must have looked at close to thirty houses in and around Asheville before narrowing it down to two. One was a cute bungalow painted yellow and the other a Victorian-era house under renovation. When I talked to the construction workers, I learned there'd been a fire. I thought of myself, drawn to relationships that needed so much work.

I asked a builder friend of Vijay's to inspect both houses. He crawled around the attic and basement, giving me a running commentary. Then we drove to the bungalow. Same scenario. At the end, his professional opinion was that the cottage was peaceful and in the best shape of any older house he'd seen. I turned to the Realtor, "I'll take it."

I am in Asheville waiting to hear if my bid has been accepted on a cottage in West Asheville. I can't sit still. My friend Robbie came to visit. Thank God. What would I do if she wasn't here? I can't believe I'm buying a house in Buncombe County in North Carolina. Robbie suggests we find some barbeque. Sounds good.

I want this house. I couldn't buy a garage in New York for this price. I'm about to start fresh. I'm scared too and can't catch my breath. It's moving so fast. What the hell! I've jumped in and now I'm ready to swim.

We end up at Little Pigs BBQ. Turned my cell phone on. Why haven't they called yet? What if I don't get it? I can't believe my luck, it's painted yellow too.

I came down to rent a place. No, *that voice inside says,* we're going to buy a house. *I'm heading for another wild ride. The best part is my heart is wide open and beating fast.*

BACK IN SEA CLIFF, MY LIFE BECAME A WHIRLWIND OF PACKING, LUNCHes, dinners, and drinks. Everyone I knew wanted to take me out to celebrate. Friends told me how much my decision to move inspired them to grab hold of their own dreams. I heard how much I was loved, how I made a difference in people's lives. I was buoyed up by their love and good wishes, filled by every word, every hug, and every kiss.

I HACKED A LENGTH OF BUBBLE WRAP AND ROLLED UP ANOTHER Venetian wine glass that I bought in TJ Maxx for $3.95. What a find! They were gorgeous, pale blue with silver trim. My friend's eyes opened wide when she saw my cart. "Do you know how much these cost at Bloomingdale's?"

Family and friends came to help. Bubble wrap littered the floor. I heard the rip as tape sealed another box.

When I left Irvington in 1980, I waited alone for the movers to come. Everything was packed. All the curtains, plants, and soft cushions that had transformed the space into a warm home were packed in boxes and I was left with an empty shell, the reality of life in a poor neighborhood.

I remembered myself on the street late one night returning from work in Manhattan, running from the man who followed me, hands holding a rope destined for my neck. In fear, I had run into the traffic coming off the Garden State Parkway exit, stumbling, almost getting hit. Running for my life.

I checked the clock. The movers were an hour late. What if they didn't show? What if I couldn't get out of Irvington? We had lived there three years, from when I left Vinny until I got a job and enough money to escape. I called the movers, men from Newark. A woman answered. Were they coming? Yeah, she said, they just left.

That was over twenty years ago.

Leaving Sea Cliff was a better story—but not an easy one. My life shattered there and again I rebuilt.

TREES

I LOOKED IN THE MIRROR A LOT BEFORE I LEFT SEA CLIFF, WONDERING what bold part of me had surfaced to entice me away from my native city? I'd done bold things before, like leaving my husband years before, but this? Who had I become that I would finally leave home at fifty-five? What I saw was the face of a woman who had made peace with her life. Her eyes were open and curious, ready for new adventure.

"Where are the trees?" was a phrase some part of me kept asking. Well, they're right here. "But no, no," the voice said, "I mean *all* the trees."

After seeing Asheville, I knew those were the trees.

I walked through my beloved Sea Cliff: walked every familiar street, every favorite house or garden that had sustained me those nine years, impressing them in my memory. At the bay, I looked across the water to the lights of Port Washington reflected in its shimmering surface. I'd come there, raw and ragged from Jeremy's illness...

I thought I'd stay forever, but I was only passing through on my way to another part of my life—a new beginning in another state.

I was finished here. Every cell of my body knew it.

I walked the field with the fir trees that I stood under so many nights, leaning against their rough bark for support. I climbed the hills, turned to see Westchester across Long Island Sound, the lights of the Throgs Neck Bridge crossing over into the Bronx and in the distance, New York City with the Twin Towers rising like two exclamation points. No matter where I was, the Towers on the horizon pointed me home—my native city.

Tremont Street, Asheville, NC—2001

GONE

The movers and my friends had left. My car was loaded and I was almost ready to go. Cuttings from my perennials were packed into my Mitsubishi Eclipse. Every inch of space was crammed with plants and provisions for the next week. I walked the empty rooms, picking up debris, paper cups, and dead plant leaves, putting them in the cardboard box I carried. I made one last turn through the scene of my last seven years.

It looked like a blank canvas or an abandoned set. Someone else would come, clean it, and repaint it. Make it theirs. I stood by the living room window high up in the attic and said goodbye to my favorite pine tree, the one the morning sun rose behind. I had watched the topmost branch grow for seven years, from a small wavering tendril to a strong new limb taking the greenness of the tree even higher.

I descended the stairs I had fallen down those many years ago as I worked with *The Artist's Way* to bring all my deepest longings to the surface. Jerry had installed a handrail after that. Now I ran my hand over its smooth surface.

The day had been hot, the hottest so far this year, and I was dirty and sweaty. I took one last shower, with no curtain, in the echoing bathroom. It felt delicious and refreshing. Dripping wet, I stared at the garden for the last time as the sun set.

As I stepped out of the tub onto the cool tile floor, I realized the towels were packed away. I searched for something to dry myself with. What I found was one of Jenny's old diapers, soft from years of washing. I dried myself with it, laughing.

I would attend one final yoga class at Elizabeth's studio before I left. Yes, tonight, after this exhausting day.

My cousin Florence and my friend Patti both offered me a place to stay for a couple of days, before the moving van arrived at my new home. But I was finished. Already gone.

By the time I left yoga class, it was after nine. I merged onto the Long Island Expressway for the last time as a New Yorker. The yoga had deepened my reflective mood and I drove the familiar roads knowing they would never have the same meaning as they did tonight.

It started to rain as I drove across the Bronx, past my childhood world, on my way to the George Washington Bridge. I thought of my family's annual walk across the bridge, how the narrow walkway jutted out. At the bridge towers, I couldn't catch my breath and had to gather courage to keep going. I'd held onto the railing and inched along, staring at the roadway, refusing to look at the Hudson's swirling waters or listen to my father yelling, "Come on!"

Tonight, I took the upper level. Traffic was light so I slowed down and gazed at Manhattan's buildings lit up like jewels in a treasure chest. The Empire State Building's spire was lost in the clouds; I couldn't see the colored lights at the top that changed with the seasons. Further down at the bottom of the island, the Twin Towers were now Manhattan's highest points, not as beautiful as the art deco Chrysler Building, but they had grown on me nevertheless until they became the beacons that showed where Manhattan was. I followed the curve of the Hudson River, outlined by car lights on the West Side Drive, as it snaked around Manhattan until it disappeared on its way to the sea.

Goodbye native city, harbor, crucible, the energy-filled chaotic scene of my life. I was headed for a new state where trees replaced buildings, with rolling mountains as my view. I thought of Jeremy, buried under three tall pine trees and knew he would approve.

It was 11:00 in the evening, July 25, 2001.

I drove New Jersey's rain-slicked highways, crossed the Delaware River into Pennsylvania with my two birds, Sweetie and Skye, on the seat beside me, rocking in their cage to the rhythm of the moving car.

The night road shimmered like a mirror. Everyone's love and hugs paved the way as I slipped out of one life into another.

I was going home.

The next morning, as I woke in the motel, I still heard rain and thought about the long drive ahead. My two birds seemed curious about where they were as I carried their cage to the car and wedged them in the front seat.

Eighteen-wheelers barreled past, spraying water on my windshield. I held my breath and clenched the wheel, unable to see the Shenandoah Mountains in the rain and mist. Disconnected—neither here nor back in New York. I'd broken free and nothing felt familiar. Exhausted, I pulled into a truck stop and fell asleep slumped over the wheel, the open window drenching me with cool rain. My birds rocked on their swings next to me. I thought they'd be upset with the changes but they preened and seemed unconcerned.

The rain continued all through Virginia. Streaks of light poured out of breaks in the clouds as I started the seven-mile descent into North Carolina. I loved to drive this stretch, swooping around the curves, passing runaway-truck ramps and trucks with grinding gears. I imagined myself a bird flying high above the cliffs with town lights far below. I had two hours until Asheville and although tired, I wasn't stopping now. I drove US 40 straight towards those green mountains, holding their image in my mind until they loomed dark against the star-filled sky.

Home. New home. I started to cry as I put my foot down on the accelerator and raced up the curves, gaining elevation, past Black Mountain. I pulled up to my new house and started unloading everything from the car—plants, cuttings from my perennials and another box of my landlord Jerry's cuttings. I set the birdcage on a box. Next, my computer, towels, pillow, everything I needed to camp out for a week until the movers came. On autopilot, I unloaded, dropping everything on the living room floor, my footsteps hollow and loud in my empty house.

FLY

In 2002, when my husband Don and I were first together, he would say, "Tell me about Jeremy." The story emerged, as I told him about my son, whom he would never meet, until he knew him as well as I had the power in my heart to tell. He took my words into his generous heart and I knew I had found the man who could hold me in all my facets. He was not afraid of my strength or my tears.

"You and Jeremy would have been great friends." I learned from my son about love and tenderness, about having the courage to face death. Jeremy taught me what kind of man I deserved. It took me years and leaving New York City to find him.

"Tell me about your son. Tell me about your life." I saw the love and happiness in Don's face when we were together. I listened to his feelings and encouraged him, something he'd never had. My story healed him as his path, so different from mine, healed me.

"Tell me about your son." Don welcomed him and I could feel Jeremy smiling. I just wished he were here to be part of this new life.

"Tell me, tell me, tell me how you came to be you?" Will we ever be finished with this story? Can we ever really know one another?

"Tell me."

Yes, I am healing; yes, I am learning trust; yes, I believe I have a right to this joy and happiness. Yes, I believe I don't have to wake up alone.

Can I let go of what I think my life is supposed to be and take in the gifts I have been given? I want to give up the old story, fly free like the birds that have been my spirit guides since I was a child in the Bronx.

HANDS

In 2008, Jenny and I held hands as we walked between rows of our friends and family in Libba and Tom's Black Mountain backyard. When we reached the front of the aisle, I kissed Jenny and took Don's hand.

Puja married us.

I think of how Vijay, a friend of Puja's that I met on my front porch in Sea Cliff, drew me down to Asheville and became a friend. I was passed from hand to loving hand on my way into a new life.

2010

HOLE

This, I miss: sending my child into his future, watching him grow, and the peace of his carrying a part of me after I am gone.

THIS I HAVE: YEARS AHEAD WITHOUT HIM. ON HIS BIRTHDAY THIS YEAR, I talked to Jenny, rambling on about new paint colors for the walls until she told me she was taking time to be by herself, and I fell into March 9 and couldn't get out. I slammed into death and it took my breath away. All I could do was aimlessly walk the streets of Asheville in the rain and think how futile it all is. My heart ached. I ate comfort food and talked to my friends, but didn't feel better. I went home and lay on the couch reading a book, hardly even responding to Don when he came home. I had nothing to give.

But the next day I felt better. I picked myself up and dusted myself off. Remembered I was alive with the many things that hold me in life.

See, There He Is

Hotchkiss, Colorado

EDGE

Don and I drove two thousand miles so I could hug my brother Jim in the driveway of his Colorado farm. Twenty years had passed since I last saw him. He looked older. So did I.

Later we went to the Black Canyon of the Gunnison. Both of us recoiled from the edge, afraid to free fall past eons of accumulated rock. The canyon was deep and narrow, the river far below. I crept to the edge, panic in my chest, every nerve on fire while he reminded me of our forced marches as children across the George Washington Bridge, both of us clinging to the railing.

"You too?" I said. "Afraid of heights?"

He nodded.

The sun was strong and beat down on us. I asked what I had come all this way to know, "What did you think of our childhood?"

"I can't remember anything."

I thought of all the times we had stood side by side. Now I realized how alone we had both felt. I put my arm around him. We held each other and walked slowly away—so much to find words for.

From where I stand, twenty years have collapsed. All the stories, drama, and loss seem oddly irrelevant. Through the window I see Queen Anne's Lace blowing in the breeze, hear the buzz of Rufous hummingbirds at the feeder and the whinny of Jim's horses in the distance. The hurts are gone and time is moving fast—he's had a heart attack.

It took me years to wrestle my hurt and betrayal, to even begin to think about calling. It's always me reaching out. Yes, I've resented it but if I don't, where will we be? It's been hard sometimes, waiting six months for a reply. I see that, despite the years since we've been together, we have similar values and views of life.

Under the surface, much is yet unsaid. I had to release my judgment to even start reaching out. I haven't seen him since our mother died, but I have had many conversations in my mind. He is a product of our family, as I am. His wife, Lynn, tells me he doesn't reach out even to her.

I'm in the yard early in the morning, walking past the sheep. The farm smells are oddly comforting. Water rushes from the irrigation ditch and speeds down to the pasture. I am at peace.

Until now I hadn't realized how much shame I carried for being estranged from my brother, as if I alone had caused it. The shame is gone now.

Twenty years I've lived, past the death of my son, tempered and changed by life until I have arrived here—fresh. Time is precious. The hurts and anger fade like mist in the early morning sun. I'm done with it all. Is this the wisdom of the years, of having grown older?

What do I hope for? A chance to heal our past and he tells me he wants it too.

The chickens call their concerned alarm as I draw closer. In the field to the left is the donkey Jim calls the Avenging Ass. We laugh a lot. Our lives have been very different, but our trajectory out of the Bronx seems similar now. Get free. Find a place where we can call the shots. Where we are not living in fear.

SHIELD

The weekend of Jenny's bridal shower in New York, I decide to visit Gate of Heaven where Jeremy is buried, usually my first stop when visiting New York. Coming down the Merritt Parkway from Robbie's house, I pull out a rusty mental map to figure which road to take—the Cross Westchester to where? I look for Valhalla, the irony not lost on me, but I miss the exit. My memory is growing fuzzy. Can I still navigate New York roads? I pull into a gas station, ask for a map, and am told they don't carry maps.

How can they not have maps?

A man looks up from pouring himself coffee and asks where I am going. I tell him. His family is buried at Gate of Heaven. After a few directions, I am off. It isn't too far. He even uses the landmark of a restaurant I remember.

I buy something for Jeremy's grave, not flowers that would die too soon, but a bluebird and a glass candle with Our Lady of Guadalupe painted on the front. I drive to his grave in the shade of the three huge pine trees.

I walk down the hill, kneel, scrape away some dirt and position the candle. I place the sweet bluebird on the bottom ledge of the tombstone. A gusty breeze makes it difficult to light the candle. Three tries before the flame catches. I cup my hands to protect the flame from the wind. I kneel like that for a long time but grow tired, take my hands away and sit back. Good news. I tell him his sister is getting married.

The candle blows out.

I light it again, cup my hands again, and watch the tiny flame flicker and take hold. I realize I can't shield the flame from the wind forever.

Jenny and Josh's Wedding, Mexico—2010

SHINE

This, Jeremy has to miss: Jenny's wedding in Mexico, my wedding to Don. I would have liked him to walk me down the aisle but Jenny did, the two of us the ones left from years ago. He will miss his first love.

This, Jenny misses: sharing memories of their childhood with Jeremy. She walks alone.

Here we are at Jenny's wedding. Yes, it has happened. My daughter is to be married, something she's wanted for years. First she had to find the right one. She tried all the dishes at the smorgasbord, some tasted good for a while, others I wondered why she didn't vomit at the first taste.

She has found a good man with a good heart. "Tall and Bald" she calls Josh. It's been five years since she brought him to my sixtieth birthday party and he stood by the door taking in the friends, the blessings, hugs, good wishes, and tears.

Here we are in Mexico, all forty-eight of us. Four sets of parents. They are both from divorced families. Jenny vows this will be her only wedding.

Blue skies and gentle breezes grace us in November. The turquoise ocean is inviting. I am the mother of the bride. What does that mean? I'm here to hold a space for Jenny, to hold her in my heart and witness her walking down the aisle in the sand on her father's arm towards the sea, towards Josh who waits tall and handsome under the canopy where they will pledge their love.

She and I have walked and walked and arrived in a better life.

There's just enough breeze and clouds to keep us cool. I sit next to Don and we hold hands and listen to the short ceremony. They exchange rings and kiss for a long time. I feel their emotions as they hold onto one another, maybe surprised to finally be here, saying YES, we do. They release butterflies that float away in the breeze; some land in our hair or on our clothes.

Two families with all our histories have come to Mexico for a party. We drink a lot of margaritas and float along. I am surprised by how much I drink, but it's been a long road and I want to dance.

I see my brother, Jim, and Lynn behind us. He didn't come to our mother's funeral or Jeremy's either, yet he's here now. Maybe weddings are easier.

We wander the hotel paths, with everything arranged to cater to us. Although at first I wasn't sure I would like the experience, I love it. Jenny and Josh deserve this lovely memory. They deserve to be celebrated and loved and cherished.

I see my ex-husband Vinny. He's aged, and this reminds me we are at the other end of life. We are here with the young ones, still alive with all our appetites, still dreaming and planning and loving. Yes, I will be here fully until I am not.

Jenny stands by her father. She is voluptuous in her bridal gown with her hair done up, more makeup than I've ever seen her wear. She looks at Josh and he smiles at her. This day is all about them—the sun and breeze, our smiling faces, the warmth, the ocean lapping at the shore. Flowers everywhere.

She takes her father's arm, leans in to say something, and he laughs, pats her arm. He is beaming. They begin to walk onto the white path strewn with rose petals. Josh waits, his arms clasped in front of him, tall and serious, waiting for her to reach him.

Sea Cliff—2011

NATIVE

A YEAR LATER IN MAY I RETURN TO SEA CLIFF. I DRIVE PAST THE POWER plant, with Hempstead Harbor a blur in the fog, up Littleworth Lane to the house I lived in with Jeremy. The owner, if he's still there, has followed true to his statement to plant a beautiful garden. Bamboo, arborvitae, and small trees form a protected space.

At dusk I drive the streets as their names come back to me—Carlton Place, Dubois Street, all the while talking to myself as I remember a particular street or house I want to see. Many are still the same colors as before, particularly a gorgeous pink Victorian on the road by Roslyn Harbor. Harmonious Homes is still there, as well as Dreams East.

I find my way in the rain to the Welwyn Preserve but drive past its locked gates to the Webb Institute. I get out at the parking lot and walk their lawn in the wind-driven rain because I can smell the salt air of Long Island Sound.

I lived here; this was my home.

Here I grounded and was healed by the beauty that surrounded me.

Lush established gardens bloom everywhere, speaking to years of nurture and tending, the slow accumulation of living while the seasons change and the clouds and rain roll by on their way to the sea.

As I walk around, I realize that Sea Cliff lives in my imagination not here ten years later, where I am a visitor. My life lies 750 miles away.

I have history here but this is not my physical home, although it may be my spiritual home. I can no more come to Sea Cliff now and experience it as I did when I first moved, than I could envision how I would become the me living in the South, not needing the solace I received here.

The next day I head for Manhattan on the Long Island Expressway, see the familiar skyline missing the Twin Towers as I approach the Queens-Midtown Tunnel. I feel the hole where they once were.

The remembered names of streets come easily to me because I am a New Yorker, a native of this vast city that holds citizens from around the world. I pay my toll, drive under the East River and onto the streets of Manhattan. I park my car, exit the garage, and flow into the stream of people. I carry my laptop across my shoulders and walk to the Union Square subway station where I purchase a MetroPass and head uptown to meet my client, a children's book publisher. Because New York in many ways remains the same, even though particular stores have changed and the crowds are different, I realize I have changed. My heart doesn't catch on old wounds.

Josh calls me on my cell phone. We talk about the surprise birthday party he is planning for Jenny.

My roots here were built upon years deeply lived. It doesn't matter if others don't remember or are gone; what matters is that it's alive in my heart and that others love its beauty.

I lived here by the ocean, surrounded by this water, this maritime land. I was a native of the coastline, native of the place where land and water meet. They were my familiars, my land, my city, the earth that I sprang from.

QUESTIONS

Before my mother was due home from work, my father would take his sentinel place at the second-floor kitchen window, watching for her car to pass, jingling the change in his pocket. If she were even a few minutes late, he would pace. What if she didn't come home, like his mother, then his father, and then his aunt—three people who died and abandoned him, all before he was five? It set the tone of his life and later, ours—how tenuous love is, how it can disappear in a heartbeat.

His routines, every penny spent written down or eating peas on Tuesday, kept him safe.

Our small one-bedroom Bronx apartment contained such unexpressed emotion, causing nightmares and violent inner storms that gripped me and twisted my mind.

I came to love my father after I moved out, when I didn't have to deal with his criticism and control anymore.

My mother pledged never to leave him, telling me years later, "We don't talk about emotions in this family."

I think of my father's many facets and why I am fascinated with him even in death. He was not an easy man to understand because he was not given to talk much. Anyway, who asked him questions during his solitary life?

He birthed a daughter filled with questions, filled with the desire to go deep, but how do you probe the depths when someone keeps the door locked?

I loved mysteries, read every library book with a skull on its spine. I could have stayed home and read my father! He taught me to hear what wasn't being said. My mother too, although her unspoken words told me she was depressed. All those words careened around that tiny apartment looking for a way out or for someone to notice them.

Many of the words found their way into my brain, seeking to string together as sentences, like crumbs that would lead me out of the woods into the cool morning light.

I went in search of the meaning of what I had heard without words. I looked in books. I looked in men, in the faces of my tiny children, searching for answers. What I found were more questions. What I found was a way into my own dark sea. I dove in with one breath and swam for years in it. Down. Down. Looking...

See, There He Is

This, I miss: Being able to introduce my son—I say this proudly because I had raised him up good—to my friends, to Don, to you. I introduce him with my words. When I write, he enters into your imagination.

See, there he is with his freckled face, his tall thin body, his lopsided grin, and goofy humor. Here he is, big-hearted and gentle, standing in the doorway with his hands in his pockets, calling the dog "Butthead."

Acknowledgments

First, I want to thank my children, Jennifer and Jeremy, for walking with me as family. Your love has healed me. Our stories are intertwined. *See, There He Is* recounts my remembrance of a time that was most profound.

Thank you to everyone who arrived at the perfect time to offer help as I wrote and rewrote.

Peggy Millin's centered writing classes provided a weekly circle of connection, support, and shared story. Peggy, you have nurtured me through the process of writing, many parts were written in your classes. Peggy, dear friend, your encouragement has helped me birth this book.

Melissa Stanz asked to read an earlier version and we met for over two years as I shared my story and she used her expertise as writer and editor to guide the story. Thank you dear friend for believing in me.

MC McIlvoy, my mentor and teacher par excellence, arrived as I was ready to take the book to the next level. Your wise, wise guidance pushed me to go deeper and deeper to bring the fullness of my story to life.

Bonnie Soniat, poet and friend, read a later version and commented with her poet's intuitive eye.

My daughter Jennifer so graciously read the book and gave me invaluable comments, love, and encouragement, reliving difficult parts of our lives with great openheartedness and generosity as only one who walked on this journey can do. Jennifer, my love for you has no end.

Jeremy, quite simply, you changed my life and taught me that love does not die

Don, my husband, who when we first met, asked me to tell him about Jeremy and spent countless hours listening as I spoke about the son he would never meet. Your love, caring, generous spirit, and sense of humor have carried me through.

My writing groups, friends, and those who have encouraged me and sat next to me as we all told our stories, I honor your strengths and friendships, our laughter and tears. You are priceless.

Friends and early readers, Robbie Helling, Karen Lauritzen, Trish Marshall, and Connie Burns, thank you for your comments and suggestions that have helped shape this book.

My parents, who despite the circumstances of their lives, gave me everything they had to give, guided me with integrity, and taught me what is important in life.

My son-in-law, Josh Letourneau, and my grandson, Declan Jeremy, who has shown me how the world looks to those who are newly born and opened me to the joy of grandparenting. Thank you both for taking me into your future.

Last, I want to honor all parents who have lost children, who have had their future taken away, and have yet risen to live a life they hadn't expected but have embraced with courage, grace, and openheartedness.

About the Author

Ginger Graziano is the creative director of Ginger Graziano Design Group, which specializes in children's educational publishing, book design, and non-profit and business collateral. She is also a sculptor, a painter, a poet, and an energy healer. She lives in Asheville, North Carolina, with her husband, Don, and two parakeets.

The author is grateful to the following journals and anthologies for publishing pieces from *See, There He Is*. "Exact Change Speeds Trips" was published in *Embodied Effigies* from Ball State University. "Sweat" was published in *Stone Voices/Shanti Arts*. "Bless the Ice Cream," "Sloan Kettering," and "Breakdown" were published in the anthology *Writing in Circles*. My poetry has been published in the following journals: "Shed" in *The Conium Review*, "Mea Culpa" in *Long Story Short*, and "Blood" in *The Great Smokies Review*.

www.ingramcontent.com/pod-product-compliance
Lightning Source LLC
Chambersburg PA
CBHW051940290426
44110CB00015B/2054